The Forgotten Witnesses to the Lives of Tudor Queens

SYLVIA BARBARA SOBERTON

Great Ladies

The Forgotten Witnesses to the Lives of Tudor Queens

Copyright © Sylvia Barbara Soberton 2017

The right of Sylvia Barbara Soberton to be identified as the Author of the Work has been asserted by her in accordance with the Copyright, Designs and Patents Act 1988.

All rights reserved. No part of this publication may be reproduced, stored in a retrieval system, or transmitted, in any form or by any means without the prior written permission of the publisher, nor be otherwise circulated in any form of binding or cover other than in which it is published and without a similar condition being imposed on the subsequent purchaser.

ISBN-13: 978-1543084924
ISBN-10: 1543084923

Contents

Prologue 1

Family trees 2

Chapter 1 "Richly beseen" 4

Chapter 2 "Of gentle birth and beautiful" 24

Chapter 3 "The damsels of her court" 43

Chapter 4 "I am a woman" 62

Chapter 5 "Old trusty women" 77

Chapter 6 "Message from the marchioness" 85

Chapter 7 "The first accusers" 94

Chapter 8 "Many ancient ladies and gentlewomen" ...103

Chapter 9 "Continuance in the King's favour" 118

Chapter 10 "Is not the Queen abed yet?" 129

Chapter 11 "Privy to all her doings" 143

Chapter 12 "A second court" 158

Chapter 13 "She went out weeping" 172

Chapter 14 "A flock of peeresses" 180

Chapter 15 "The Queen's most intimate confidantes" ..193

Chapter 16 "Harbour of honourable gentlewomen" ...201

Chapter 17 "Her most intimate Lady of the Bedchamber" ...222

Chapter 18 "In the prince's court" 233

Chapter 19 "Such a She Wolf" 240

Chapter 20 "Flouting Wenches" 249

Picture section 263
Selected Bibliography.. 284

PROLOGUE

There has been a great deal written about Tudor queens, but less so about those women who surrounded the throne, who may have held even more power and influence than those who actually wore the golden crown.

Some ladies who served at the Tudor court are only faceless silhouettes lost to the sands of time, but there are those who dedicated their lives to please their royal mistresses and left documentation, allowing us to piece their life stories together and link them to the stories of Tudor queens. These female attendants saw their queens and princesses up close and often used their intimate bonds to their own benefit. Some were beloved, others hated.

This is the story of the ladies of the Tudor court like you've never read it before.

FAMILY TREES

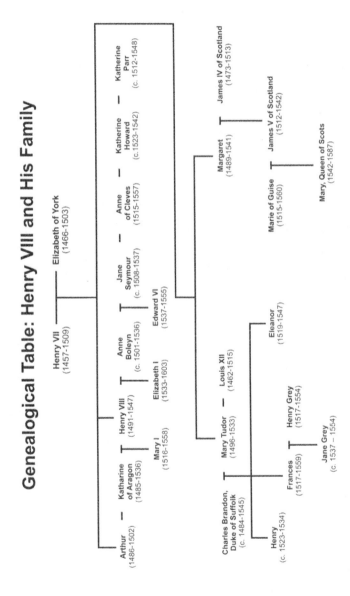

Family trees

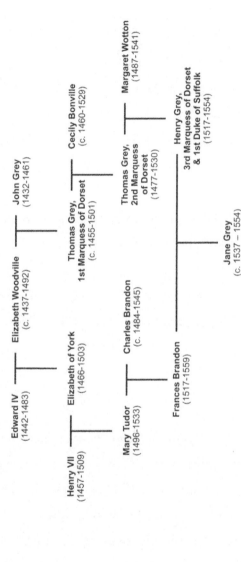

CHAPTER 1
"RICHLY BESEEN"

With the marriage of Henry VII to Elizabeth of York on 18 January 1486, England gained a new Queen. Like her mother, Elizabeth Woodville, Elizabeth of York was a native Englishwoman, but, unlike her, she was of blood royal. Some even believed that Elizabeth of York had a far better claim to the throne than her husband, "the unknown Welshman" who won the battle of Bosworth and toppled the last Yorkist King, Richard III. Henry arranged his own coronation on 30 October 1485 to emphasize that he was the King in his own right and not because he was to marry the eldest daughter of Edward IV. In the late sixteenth century, Francis Bacon would sum up the feelings of many Englishmen by saying that Henry's victory at Bosworth gave him the knee of his subjects, but that his marriage to Elizabeth secured their hearts.

Henry VII had spent fourteen years in exile, and when he was crowned, observers noted that his mother, the formidable Lady Margaret Beaufort, Countess of Richmond, "wept marvellously" watching her son become the King of England. These tears were fully justified. She fought hard to see her son safely back in England, but she also knew that kings were easily toppled from their thrones, as illustrated by

"Richly beseen"

the example of Richard III. Henry's defeat of Richard was the beginning of a lifelong struggle to win the loyalty of his new, distrusting English subjects.

"He is disliked", wrote the Spanish envoy Pedro de Ayala in 1498.[1] Indeed, the ambassador observed that Henry wanted to rule "in the French fashion" but was unable to do so because the English were not used to such a model of kingship. To them, Henry was a foreigner brought up abroad and "not a great man". His wish to employ foreigners in his service reflected his suspicions about his English subjects, whose envy was, according to de Ayala, "diabolical" and "without equal". De Ayala also observed that the King's firstborn son, Prince Arthur, was beloved because he was "the grandchild of his grandfather".[2] Indeed, Edward IV, Elizabeth of York's father, was much beloved, and his reign was still a fresh memory. Two Bohemian visitors who were guests at Edward's court and witnessed the churching ceremony of his wife after Elizabeth of York was born in 1466 recorded that Edward IV was "a handsome, upstanding man" and had "the most splendid court that could be found in all Christendom."[3]

Elizabeth of York was seventeen when her father died suddenly in 1483, and she remembered his court well. Edward IV practiced the politics of ostentation, accentuating his regal status through clothing and a display of magnificence. The King had spent a short time in exile in Burgundy in 1471 and decided to model his court and fashions on the Burgundian style when he returned to England:

"He was usually dressed in a variety of costly clothes, in quite another fashion than we had seen before in our time. The sleeves of his cloak hung in ample folds like those of a monk's frock, lined inside with the richest furs and rolled on the shoulders. Thus the prince, who was of imposing build, taller than others, presented a novel and remarkable spectacle."[4]

He was well aware that his appearance overawed spectators, and Edward often "called to his side complete strangers, when he thought that they had come with the intention of addressing or beholding him more closely".[5] His court became the epitome of magnificence:

"You might have seen, in those days, the royal court presenting no other appearance than such as fully befits a most mighty kingdom, filled with riches and with people of almost all nations, and boasting of those the most sweet and beautiful children."[6]

No wonder, then, that Elizabeth of York quickly gained popularity as her father's heiress and became the embodiment of reconciliation. In creating the Tudor rose—the symbol of the two unified dynasties and an icon of the newly formed dynasty—Henry VII used Elizabeth's white rose of York and

"Richly beseen"

surrounded it with the outer petals of the red Lancastrian rose.

Elizabeth quickly settled into the traditional role of a medieval queen, surrounding herself with her ladies-in-waiting, who accompanied her everywhere she went. Henry VII realized that good-looking, beautifully arrayed and well-mannered women added splendour to his court, and he insisted that his wife's ladies "should be of gentle birth and beautiful".[7] The most prominent among Elizabeth of York's ladies-in-waiting were her younger sisters, who performed key roles during occasions of state, such as the christening of Elizabeth's firstborn son, Arthur, in 1486 and her coronation in 1487. Edward IV and Elizabeth Woodville had seven daughters: Elizabeth, Mary, Cecily, Margaret, Anne, Katherine and Bridget. Two of them died before reaching adolescence; Margaret in 1472 at the age of eighth months and Mary in 1482 at the age of fifteen. After their father's death in April 1483, the girls were taken by their mother to the sanctuary at Westminster Abbey.

Elizabeth Woodville feared the influence of her husband's brother, Richard, Duke of Gloucester, who intercepted Edward IV's eldest son, the young Edward V, on his way to London. Richard demanded that Elizabeth surrender her second son, whom she had taken to sanctuary, Richard, Duke of York. She parted with him very unwillingly

Great Ladies

and was soon to regret her decision. Although Richard of Gloucester assured Elizabeth that Edward would be crowned, he proclaimed him illegitimate and thus unfit to inherit. Richard proclaimed himself King of England and was crowned as Richard III on 6 July 1483. Elizabeth Woodville's sons were seen "more rarely behind the bars and windows of the Tower", where they were placed "until at length they ceased to appear altogether".[8]

Richard III's first parliament declared Elizabeth Woodville's marriage to Edward IV invalid due to Edward's earlier alleged pre-contract with another woman, and all of their children were thus deemed illegitimate. By March 1484, Richard had reached out to his brother's widow and pledged that he would provide for her daughters and would arrange respectable marriages for all of them if they agreed to leave sanctuary. Elizabeth Woodville saw no other option but to trust the new King. But there were more pressing matters on Richard III's mind, and in the end he arranged only one marriage—that of Cecily of York to Ralph Scrope, "an obscure man of no reputation", according to the first Tudor historian Polydore Vergil.[9] This marriage was annulled after Richard III was defeated at Bosworth.

Henry VII saw his wife's sisters as marriageable pawns, and his first parliament proclaimed them legitimate again. He made sure that they were prominent figures during

"Richly beseen"

court ceremonies. One of such grand state occasions was the christening of Prince Arthur on 24 September 1486. As the eldest sister, Cecily of York was given the privilege of carrying the newly born prince to the baptismal font:

"After them [the lords] my Lady Cecily, the Queen's eldest sister, bare the Prince wrapped in a mantle of crimson cloth of gold furred with ermine, with a train, which was borne by my Lady the Marchioness of Dorset".[10]

The following year Cecily played an important role during Elizabeth of York's coronation, which took place on 25 November 1487, two years after Henry VII's accession. Coronations in medieval England were held on a Sunday and were the culmination of a three-day cycle of elaborately staged events, starting with the monarch's arrival at the Tower, a procession through the City of London to Westminster and the coronation itself. Elizabeth of York left Greenwich Palace on 23 November, accompanied by Margaret Beaufort, her mother-in-law, and "many other great estates, both lords and ladies richly beseen".[11] The Queen boarded the magnificently decorated royal barge that was to convey her to the Tower; interestingly, at this stage neither the Queen's mother nor her sisters accompanied her.

The next day, 24 November, the Queen, dressed in white cloth of gold, made her way from the Tower to

Westminster. Cecily of York bore Elizabeth's long train before the Queen climbed into an open litter, wherein she travelled through the clean-swept streets of London, decorated with tapestries hanging down from the windows of its citizens. In a chariot behind Elizabeth of York's litter travelled two women who were very close to the Queen: her sister Cecily and her maternal aunt Katherine Woodville, Duchess of Bedford. They were among the most prominent ladies and had their own female servants travelling behind them.

On 25 November 1487, Elizabeth of York went to her coronation "apparelled in a kirtle and mantle of purple velvet furred with ermines" with "a circlet of gold richly garnished with pearls and precious stones" on her head.[12] Cecily again treaded behind her, holding the long train of Elizabeth's gown. The "ray cloth" on which the Queen was walking was a coveted prize, and many people wanted to snip off a piece of it as a souvenir. This led to turmoil; "there was so much people inordinately pressing to cut the ray cloth that certain persons in the press were slain, and the order of the ladies following the Queen was broken and troubled".[13] Despite this disturbing incident, Elizabeth of York proceeded to the abbey accompanied by her ladies and the leading peers of the realm, who carried the royal insignia. The Queen's paternal uncle John de la Pole, Duke of Suffolk, carried a gilt sceptre; William FitzAlan, Earl of Arundel, carried the rod with the dove, and

"Richly beseen"

Jasper Tudor, Duke of Bedford—Henry VII's uncle and husband of Katherine Woodville—bore the crown. Elizabeth of York was then solemnly anointed and crowned as Queen Elizabeth of England.

Elizabeth of York's coronation, two years after her husband's and a year after the birth of her first son, was calculated to indicate that Henry VII's claim to the throne was not dependent on his wife being the daughter and heiress of Edward IV. From the outset, the King intended Elizabeth to play no political role and kept her short of money so that she was always dependant on his charity. The Spanish ambassador Pedro de Ayala observed that "the Queen is beloved because she is powerless".

Indeed, it was Henry VII's mother, Margaret Beaufort, who was the real power behind the throne. "The King is much influenced by his mother and his followers in affairs of personal interest and in others", remarked the perceptive Spanish ambassador, adding that "the Queen, as is generally the case, does not like it".[14] The private correspondence between Henry VII and Margaret Beaufort supports this statement. In one of her surviving letters to Henry, Margaret variously addressed her son as "my dearest and only desired joy in this world" and "dear heart". Writing on the anniversary of Henry's birth, Margaret reminisced that it was "this day of St Anne's that I did bring into this world my good and gracious prince, king and only beloved son."[15] Henry had similarly warm feelings for Margaret; he addressed her as "my most entirely well-beloved Lady and Mother" and signed himself as "your humble and loving son".[16] Unfortunately, no letters from Henry to Elizabeth survive, so we do not know if he was equally tender with his wife.

The relationship between Henry VII and Elizabeth of York has always been shrouded in mystery. There is evidence from the later part of his reign that they shared a close relationship, but it is likely that their early years were far from happy. Like most medieval marriages, theirs also started as a political arrangement. In December 1483, in the cathedral in Rennes, Henry swore an oath promising to marry Elizabeth and began planning an invasion of England. Henry naturally feared that unless he married Elizabeth of York or one of her sisters, large droves of his supporters would desert him. He was loath to admit later in his reign that many people rallied behind him because they wanted to see Edward IV's daughter on the throne. Writing in the late sixteenth century, Francis Bacon observed that Henry's "aversion towards the house of York was so predominant in him as it found place not only in his wars and councils, but in his chamber and bed". Bacon insinuated that Henry was not the most doting of husbands, adding:

"Richly beseen"

"And it is true that all his lifetime, while the Lady Elizabeth lived with him (for she died before him), he showed himself no very indulgent husband towards her, though she was beautiful, gentle and fruitful."[17]

It may be that rumours about Richard III's planned marriage to Elizabeth of York, which broke out in England and abroad in 1485, disheartened Henry and prejudiced him against Elizabeth. Indeed, Polydore Vergil, Henry VII's official and very first historian, affirmed that these rumours "pinched Henry by the very stomach" because he feared that his allies would forsake his cause if he failed to marry one of the daughters of Edward IV.[18] This suggests that Henry believed the rumours about Richard III's intended marriage to Elizabeth and assumed that Elizabeth was willing to marry her own uncle. At this point, the second eldest daughter of Edward IV, Cecily of York, was already married, and the other York princesses were far too young to be espoused. Henry was so disheartened that he contemplated marrying Katherine Herbert, the daughter of his erstwhile guardian, but was convinced not to give up on his marriage to Elizabeth. On 30 March 1485, Richard III denied rumours that he had ever contemplated marrying his niece, and five months later he was slain by Henry Tudor's forces at the battle of Bosworth.

The early years of their marriage were tainted by Henry's distrust of Elizabeth's Yorkist relatives. In February

1487, the Queen's mother, Elizabeth Woodville, was deprived of all her possessions and allocated a modest pension of four hundred marks per year, three hundred marks fewer than she received during Richard III's reign. She also withdrew to Bermondsey Abbey. The reason behind this was, according to Polydore Vergil, the fact that the Dowager Queen made peace with Richard III back in 1484 when she agreed to leave sanctuary with her daughters. Vergil argued that by leaving sanctuary, Elizabeth Woodville broke her promise "to those (mainly of the nobility) who had, at her own most urgent entreaty, forsaken their own English property and fled to Henry in Brittany, the latter having pledged himself to her elder daughter, Elizabeth". Chronicler Edward Hall was even sharper in his condemnation of Elizabeth and recorded that her "double dealings" endangered Henry's cause at the time.[19] Yet it was a strange thing to condemn the Dowager Queen for something she did three years earlier. Francis Bacon, writing in the late sixteenth century, linked this particular event with the Lambert Simnel conspiracy that broke out in 1486. Lambert Simnel was a young boy who had been groomed to impersonate Edward Plantagenet, Earl of Warwick, the son of George, Duke of Clarence. Those who wanted to see the Yorks reinstated turned to rebellion. The young Warwick was in the King's custody at the time, and Henry VII was well aware that the rebellion was aimed at deposing him. One of the leading rebels was John de la Pole, Earl of Lincoln, Elizabeth of York's

"Richly beseen"

first cousin, who was killed during the Battle of Stoke Field on 16 June 1487. Bacon believed that Elizabeth Woodville was the driving force behind this, although he admitted it was his conjecture rather than a fact based on reading primary sources. Many historians since have pointed out that Elizabeth Woodville had no reason to join the rebellion aimed at deposing her son-in-law and depriving her daughter and grandson of their royal inheritance. It seems more reasonable that Henry VII planned to seize his mother-in-law's lands to dower his wife.[20]

Yet it is also possible that Henry VII desired to avoid the embarrassment of his mother having to defer to the Queen Dowager. Before her son became King, Margaret Beaufort served as Elizabeth Woodville's lady-in-waiting; she was last recorded as carrying Bridget of York, the youngest of Elizabeth's children, to the baptismal font in 1480. The courtly protocol dictated that a crowned Queen should take precedence over other ladies of the court, and Elizabeth Woodville, mother of the current royal consort and herself a crowned Queen, had every right to take precedence over Margaret Beaufort. There is evidence that Margaret would oppose being superseded by Elizabeth Woodville during court ceremonies. Henry VII was eager to emphasize that he was King in his own right and not because he was married to the Yorkist heiress; it follows that he would be eager to have his mother, and not the mother of his wife, to be prominent at court.

Margaret adopted a semi-regal style and invented the title of My Lady the King's Mother to emphasize her new status. Her manor at Collyweston, which she remodelled, boasted a set of splendidly decorated rooms, one of them being the "Queen's chamber", which she occupied.[21] She also began to use the royal style "Margaret R." instead of the earlier signature "M. Richmond". The "R" stood for "Richmond", as in Countess of Richmond, but it could also be read as "Regina", meaning "Queen" in Latin.

Margaret was often at court, especially during the early years of her son's reign, and constantly accompanied the King and Queen. She usually deferred to Elizabeth of York, allowing her to take precedence, but she would never miss a chance to emphasize her semi-regal status as the King's mother. During the Christmas celebrations in 1488, for instance, Margaret was dressed "in like mantle and surcoat as the Queen, with a rich coronet on her head, and walking aside the Queen's half train".[22] It is notable that Margaret did not walk behind the Queen, but beside her to emphasize that she felt she was her equal. What Elizabeth of York felt about her mother-in-law's constant presence remains unknown, but she must have been frustrated at times. The Spanish ambassador recorded that although she was generally "much beloved" in

"Richly beseen"

England, she was "kept in subjection by the mother of the King"; he also recorded that she did not like the fact that her husband deferred to his mother's judgment.[23] On one occasion, Margaret dismissed a yeoman of the crown, John Hewyk, from the Queen's presence, which prompted him to remark bitterly that "he had spoken with the Queen's Grace, and should have spoken more with her said Grace, had it not been for that strong whore the King's mother".[24]

Elizabeth of York's mother was a rare guest at court, but the Queen, who had a strong feeling of family obligation, surrounded herself with her female relatives, who formed part of her train. Among the most prominent ladies of the court, apart from the Queen's sisters, were her aunts Katherine Woodville, Duchess of Bedford, and Mary FitzLewis, Countess of Rivers, as well as Elizabeth Stafford, the Queen's first cousin.

Katherine Woodville was one of the sisters of Elizabeth of York's mother. She first married Henry Stafford, second Duke of Buckingham, with whom she had several children. Buckingham was Richard III's erstwhile supporter turned traitor, who led a failed rebellion against the King and was executed for it in 1483. After Henry VII's accession, Katherine married Jasper Tudor, Henry VII's uncle, who stood by him during the years of exile and became the pillar of his nephew's reign. Jasper was awarded with the title of the Duke of

Great Ladies

Bedford. Mary FitzLewis, Countess of Rivers, was the wife of Elizabeth Woodville's brother Anthony, who was executed on Richard III's orders on 25 June 1483 in Pontefract Castle. Born on 30 May 1467, Mary was of similar age to the Queen and was favoured by playing a prominent role during the banquet that followed Elizabeth of York's coronation. According to one contemporary, Anthony Woodville was "always considered a kind, serious and just man, and one tested by every vicissitude of life. Whatever his prosperity, he had injured nobody, though benefitting many".[25] He was highly regarded by his sister and Edward IV and had been appointed governor of the Prince of Wales's household. Anthony's execution was seen as unjust by many. Elizabeth of York was seventeen at the time of Anthony's execution and must have been fond of her uncle since, twenty years after his death, in December 1502, she rewarded "a man of Pontefract" who said that Anthony had lodged in his house "at the time of his death".[26]

Among the highest paid of Elizabeth of York's attendants was her first cousin Elizabeth Stafford, daughter of Katherine Woodville; in 1502, she received a salary of £33.6s.8d.[27] She must have been regarded as the Queen's chief lady and confidante since she was appointed as chief mourner during Elizabeth of York's funeral in 1503.

The new Spanish ambassador, Rodrigo de Puebla, recorded in 1488 that the Queen had thirty-two ladies-in-

"Richly beseen"

waiting attending her in private. These "companions of angelical appearance" made a lasting impact on the ambassador.[28] Apart from good looks, the Queen's ladies were expected to be of gentle birth, accomplished in courtly merriments such as dancing, singing and playing instruments as well as being skilled needlewomen. These women surrounded Elizabeth of York at all times, but most prominently during the Queen's numerous confinements.

One of the main duties of a royal consort was bearing children. Like every other great event, childbirth was subject to elaborate ritual. About a month before the expected birth, the Queen underwent the process of "taking to her chamber", withdrawing from court life to endure her confinement. Men were not allowed to invade this all-female sanctum. Instead of the usually appointed male officers, women were to temporarily perform their tasks. They were to serve as "butlers, panters (keepers of the pantry), sewers, carvers, cup bearers; and all manner of officers shall bring to them all manner of things to the great chamber door".[29] When she was pregnant for the second time, it was recorded that:

"Upon All Hollow's Eve [1489], the Queen took [to] her chamber at Westminster, greatly accompanied with ladies and gentlewomen; that is to say, the Lady the King's mother, the Duchess of Norfolk and many others, having before her the great part of the nobles of this realm present at this

Parliament. She was led by the Earl of Oxford and the Earl of Derby. The Reverent Father in God, the Bishop of Exeter, sang the Mass in pontifical robes, and after Agnus Dei. Then the Queen was led as before. The Earls of Shrewsbury and of Kent held the towel when the Queen took her rites, and the torches were held by knights. And after Mass, accompanied as before, when she was come into her great chamber, she stood under her Cloth of Estate. Then there was ordained a void of spices and sweet wine. That done, my Lord the Queen's Chamberlain in very good words desired in the Queen's name, the people there present to pray God to send her the good hour [safe delivery]."[30]

On 28 November 1489, Elizabeth of York gave birth to a daughter, who was named Margaret after the King's mother. Four more children followed in quick succession: Henry (the future Henry VIII) in 1491, Elizabeth in 1492, Mary in 1496 and Edmund in 1499. Edmund and Elizabeth, who was named after Elizabeth Woodville, died in early childhood.

Elizabeth Woodville died on 8 June 1492 while her daughter was in confinement. According to her last will, the Dowager Queen had "no worldly goods" to bequeath to "the Queen's Grace, my dearest daughter". She expressed her regret that she could not "reward any of my children, according to my heart and mind" and beseeched God to "bless her Grace, with all her noble issue, and with as good heart and

"Richly beseen"

mind as is to me possible, I give her Grace my blessing, and all the aforesaid my children".[31] Elizabeth requested a humble funeral "without pompous entering or costly expenses done thereabout."[32] Her wishes were respected, and she was buried during a low-key ceremony when her body was conveyed from Bermondsey Abbey to Windsor "without ringing of any bells or receiving of the dean or canons in their habits". The herald who recorded the funeral was dismayed at the lack of proper ceremonial. The Dowager Queen's hearse was "such as they use for the common people".[33]

In stark contrast to Elizabeth Woodville's poverty, Margaret Beaufort lived in opulence. By 1499, she had withdrawn from court and set up her own semi-regal household at her favourite residence at Collyweston. Although married, the King's mother undertook a vow of chastity while her husband was still alive, desiring a quiet life away from the court's bustle. Apart from male officers, Lady Margaret surrounded herself with a number of noblewomen who served as her ladies-in-waiting and companions. The King's mother had a deep sense of obligation towards the ladies who became as close to her as family members, and she often distributed various gifts among them. Such valuables were treasured and treated as family heirlooms. Writing her last will in 1518, Elizabeth Neville, Lady Scrope, bequeathed "a primer and a psalter, which I had of the gift of King Henry VII's mother" to

Great Ladies

her sister Lucy.[34] Many women found comfortable reception within the Beaufort household; some ladies, like Cecily of York and Mary FitzLewis, Dowager Countess of Rivers, had rooms reserved in Margaret's spacious residence, which means they must have been frequent visitors.

NOTES

[1] *Calendar of State Papers, Spain,* Volume 1, 1485-1509, n. 209.
[2] Ibid.
[3] Malcolm Henry Ikin Letts, *The Travels of Leo of Rozmital,* p. 47.
[4] Antonia Gransden, *Historical Writing in England,* p. 271.
[5] Dominic Mancini, *The Usurpation of Richard III,* p. 65.
[6] Alec Reginald Myers, *The Household of Edward IV,* p. 48.
[7] *Calendar of State Papers, Spain,* Volume 1, n. 268.
[8] Dominic Mancini, *The Usurpation of Richard III,* p. 95.
[9] *Three Books of Polydore Vergil's English History,* Volume 29, p. 215.
[10] John Leland, *Collectanea,* Volume 4, p. 217.
[11] Ibid., p. 218.
[12] Ibid., p. 212.
[13] Ibid., p. 223.
[14] *Calendar of State Papers, Spain,* Volume 1, 1485-1509, n. 210.
[15] Mary Anne Everett Wood, *Letters of Royal and Illustrious Ladies of Great Britain,* Volume 1, pp. 119-20.
[16] Henry Ellis, *Original Letters Illustrative of English History,* Volume 1, pp. 43, 45.
[17] Francis Bacon, *Bacon: The History of the Reign of King Henry VII and Selected Works,* p. 20.
[18] *Three Books of Polydore Vergil's English History,* Volume 29, p. 215.
[19] Alison Weir, *Elizabeth of York: The First Tudor Queen,* pp. 241-42.
[20] Ibid.
[21] E.M.G. Routh, *Lady Margaret: A Memoir of Margaret Beaufort,* p. 77.
[22] John Leland, *Collectanea,* Volume 4, p. 236.
[23] *Calendar of State Papers, Spain,* Volume 1, 1485-1509, n. 205, 209.
[24] Alison Weir, *Elizabeth of York: The First Tudor Queen,* p. 204.
[25] Dominic Mancini, *The Usurpation of Richard III,* p. 69.
[26] Sir Nicholas Harris Nicolas, *Privy Purse Expenses of Elizabeth of York,* p. 78.

[27] Ibid., p. 99.

[28] *Calendar of State Papers, Spain*, Volume 1, 1485-1509, n. 21.

[29] Kim M. Philips, *Medieval Maidens: Young Women and Gender in England, 1270-1540*, pp. 116-7.

[30] Arlene Okerlund, *Elizabeth of York*, p. 109.

[31] John Nichols, *A Collection of All the Wills*, pp. 350-51.

[32] Ibid.

[33] Arlene Okerlund, *Elizabeth: England's Slandered Queen*, pp. 257-59.

[34] Nicholas Harris Nicolas, *Testamenta Vetusta*, Volume 2, p. 588.

CHAPTER 2
"OF GENTLE BIRTH AND BEAUTIFUL"

In 1488, negotiations opened for the marriage between Elizabeth of York's firstborn son, Arthur, Prince of Wales, and the Spanish Infanta Katharine of Aragon, daughter of Ferdinand of Aragon and Isabella of Castile. The alliance between England and Spain was prestigious and highly sought after by Henry VII, who saw it as means of adding an air of legitimacy to his newly created dynasty. Yet the "Catholic Rulers", as Ferdinand and Isabella were dubbed by the pope, "bearing in mind what happens every day to the Kings of England", had certain reservations about sending their youngest daughter to be married to Henry VII's heir.[1] Their reservations were justified. Henry was the first Tudor monarch and by no means safe on the throne. His reign was bedevilled by pretenders such as Perkin Warbeck, who emerged from obscurity in 1491 claiming to have been Queen Elizabeth of York's younger brother, Richard, Duke of York, one of the Princes in the Tower who disappeared in 1483.

Warbeck was finally captured in 1497, and surprisingly, he was not executed, but placed at court, where

"Of gentle birth and beautiful"

he was allowed to mingle freely among the courtiers. Shortly after his capture, the Venetian ambassador reported that he had seen Perkin "in a chamber of the King's palace and habitation". "He is a well favoured young man, twenty-three years old, and his wife a very handsome woman", the ambassador observed, adding that "the King treats them well, but did not allow them to sleep together".[2] Perkin's wife was Katherine Gordon, daughter of the Earl of Huntly. She was a native Scotchwoman and married Perkin in 1495 when he arrived in Scotland and dazzled her kinsman, King James III. Whether she believed that Perkin Warbeck was the lost prince and thus the rightful heir to the English throne remains unclear; she may have been convinced by the air of royal majesty surrounding Perkin, who, by all accounts, was a handsome young man who managed to win the support of several crowned heads of Europe.

Among the most high profile figures supporting his claim was Margaret of York, Dowager Duchess of Burgundy, who was the sister of Edward IV and Richard of York's aunt. In her letter written to Queen Isabella of Castile in 1492, Margaret explained that when she first saw Perkin, she "recognised him as easily as if I had last seen him yesterday or the day before (for I had seen him once long ago in England)".[3] Some contemporaries even suggested that Perkin was either Margaret's illegitimate son or a boy she groomed to overthrow

Great Ladies

Henry VII. It has been credibly suggested that a boy named Jehan le Sage, whom Margaret of York adopted when he was five years old in 1478, was raised by her to become Perkin Warbeck and claim the English throne.[4]

Whatever the truth behind Perkin Warbeck's true identity, Henry VII decided to place his wife, Katherine Gordon, in the household of Elizabeth of York. The King believed that Katherine was deceived by Perkin and never referred to her as the pretender's wife in state documents. According to certain contemporary reports, Henry VII "began a little to fantasize her person" because she was "singularly beautiful".[5] The King also made sure that Katherine was confronted with her husband, whom Henry exposed as a fraud. Warbeck was forced to admit that "he was not who he said he was" and asked for Katherine's forgiveness. She responded by bursting into tears and berating Warbeck for carrying out his deceit and separating her from her Scottish family. "I see nothing before me but death, since my chastity is lost", she bemoaned.[6]

But Henry VII was eager to treat the pretender's wife with due honours. As the kinswoman of James III of Scotland, with whom Henry wished to ally, Katherine was treated with respect and kindness. Shortly after Warbeck's capture, Henry sent her "accompanied with a goodly sort of matrons . . . to London to the Queen".[7] Elizabeth of York appointed Katherine

"Of gentle birth and beautiful"

Gordon as her lady-in-waiting, and the King settled upon her "a very honourable allowance for the support of her estate". She was nicknamed "the White Rose" because she was very beautiful.[8] Henry VII supplied items of clothing for Katherine, taking care that she appeared magnificently arrayed, as befitted the King of Scotland's kinswoman.

The parents of Katharine of Aragon, the Spanish infanta who was affianced to Prince Arthur, demanded the execution of Perkin Warbeck and Edward Plantagenet, Earl of Warwick. Ferdinand of Aragon and Isabella of Castile perceived these two young men as threats to Henry VII's throne. Ferdinand was heard saying that he would not send his daughter "to one who was not secure in his own kingdom".[9] Henry VII hesitated; Warbeck, being a native of Tournai, was not his subject, and the King would probably have been content with perpetually locking him up in the Tower. Warwick constituted a different kind of threat. He was the son of George Plantagenet, Duke of Clarence, and thus Edward IV's nephew, "the sole male descendant remaining in this branch of the family".[10] Many saw him as the rightful heir to the Yorkist throne, and people often used Warwick as a figurehead for rebellion. Henry VII decided that the establishment of his new dynasty was more important than the lives of Warbeck and Warwick, who were both executed in November 1499. Thus Henry VII cleared the way for his heir's marriage to Katharine of Aragon—a marriage that the Spanish infanta later declared had been "made in blood".[11] After the executions, the Spanish ambassador Rodrigo de Puebla exultantly reported to Ferdinand and Isabella that "there does not remain a drop of doubtful royal blood" in England except "the true blood of the King, the Queen and, above all, of the Prince of Wales".[12]

With Warbeck's and Warwick's deaths, Henry VII and Elizabeth of York could turn their attention to more pleasant matters, such as planning the festivities for Katharine of Aragon's arrival. On 16 June 1500, de Puebla reported that "the King and Queen wish very much that the ladies who are to accompany the Princess of Wales should be of gentle birth and beautiful, or at least that none of them should be ugly".[13] Henry VII debated the matter of "the servants who are to accompany the Princess of Wales" with his council, and they wished that Katharine of Aragon would arrive with as small a number of servants as possible because she "will be attended and obeyed and loved by the first noblemen and ladies of the kingdom".[14] It was agreed that most of Katharine's entourage would be sent to Spain after her wedding to Prince Arthur. By October 1500, it was agreed that among Katharine of Aragon's female servants would be "a noble matron, who would be a widow", "three ladies of noble rank who were virgins" and "a lady to act as a porter".[15] Katharine and her large entourage

"Of gentle birth and beautiful"

finally arrived in England on 2 October 1501. Dona Elvira Manuel, "a noble matron", held the position of "first lady of honour and first lady of the bedchamber" and had her own lady-in-waiting, Martina Mudarra, and two other female servants required by her high rank; she was a stickler for etiquette who would rule Katharine's household with an iron rod. Catalina Cardenas was a lady-in-waiting who attended Katharine of Aragon in her private chambers and supervised the other maids of honour. Among her "ladies of honour" were Francisca de Silva, Martina de Salazar, and Beatriz, "daughter of Dona Blanca". One of the female servants who would become Katharine of Aragon's close friend was Ines de Venegas, daughter of Dona Ines, who served as "the nurse of the Princess of Wales". Catalina de Montoya served as the Lady of Company to the maids of honour. "Daughter of Ines De Albornoz", whose name was unrecorded, and Catalina Fortes, "niece of the treasurer Morales", were to serve "in the rooms of the Princess", while two unnamed slaves were to attend the maids of honour.[16] It is clear that the list is incomplete; one of the women conspicuously absent from it was Maria de Salinas, Katharine of Aragon's dear friend, who would stay with her in England and serve her almost until the end of Katharine's life in 1536.

The long anticipated marriage between Katharine of Aragon and Prince Arthur took place on 14 November 1501 amid lavish celebrations and elaborately staged pageants. Later that evening, the couple was ceremoniously put to bed in their nuptial chamber. The act of consummation of the marriage was not witnessed by the members of the court, and the wedding night itself would later become an issue weighed in court.[17] Soon after the wedding, Henry VII decided to send the young couple to Ludlow Castle in the Welsh Marches, where the fifteen-year-old Prince Arthur was to complete his education and learn how to govern his principality.

Among the ladies who followed the Prince and Princess of Wales to Ludlow was Margaret, sister of the executed Earl of Warwick and wife of Richard Pole, chamberlain of Prince Arthur's newly formed household. Born in 1473, Margaret witnessed the most crucial events of the newly established regime, such as the christening of Prince Arthur in 1486 and the coronation of Elizabeth of York the following year. Royal by birth, she was one of the most important ladies of high rank in the kingdom and one of the last Plantagenets at the Tudor court. Katharine of Aragon soon learned that her father had demanded the execution of Margaret's brother before she arrived in England, and she was horrified. Feelings of guilt over the Earl of Warwick's unjust execution pushed Katharine to seek Margaret's friendship. Many years later, Margaret's son, Reginald Pole, recorded that Katharine was "very much bound to recompense and requite

"Of gentle birth and beautiful"

us [the Pole family] for the detriment we had received on her account (although she was not in the least to blame for it), and to show us every kindness, having found by experience that in all her sorrows and afflictions, from no family of the realm had she ever received greater consolation than from ours, although for her sake we had received so many injuries".[18]

Katharine of Aragon's time as Princess of Wales came to an abrupt end when Prince Arthur died on 2 April 1502 of "great sickness" raging in the Ludlow area.[19] Katharine was soon ordered to leave the Welsh Marches behind and return to London, where her fate was to be decided. Arthur, his parents' favourite child and the bright hope of the dynasty, perished at the age of merely sixteen. The future of the Tudors now rested on the shoulders of the eleven-year-old Henry, Duke of York, but before Henry could become his brother's successor as Prince of Wales and his father's heir apparent, Katharine needed to prove that she was not pregnant with Arthur's child. Soon it became apparent that Katharine was not pregnant, and by July 1502 her first lady of honour, Dona Elvira, informed her parents that Katharine "remains as she was here".[20] In other words, Katharine was still a virgin. Isabella of Castile made it clear that she wished Dona Elvira's soothing presence in her daughter's household at this difficult time. She instructed her ambassador to "take care that Dona Elvira remain with her, and any other persons whom she may wish

Great Ladies

to retain, according to the number which was agreed upon for her service."[21]

Upon Arthur's death, Elizabeth of York told Henry VII that they were still young and could produce more sons. The Queen was now thirty-six years old, and the King was nine years her senior. Elizabeth soon discovered that she was pregnant again. In November 1502, she interviewed and rewarded one French nurse who visited her in Baynard's Castle, and another nurse, Mistress Harcourt, who conferred with the Queen at Westminster "by the labour of Dame Kateryn Grey".[22] The Lady Kateryn Grey was often accorded a place of honour during occasions of state and was a constant presence during the Queen's private moments; she seems to have been one of Elizabeth of York's favourite ladies. The inscription on her tomb states that she was lady-in-waiting to Elizabeth Woodville before she entered the service of Elizabeth of York; Kateryn may have been favoured because she was a precious link to the Queen's mother.[23] The inscription also states that she was a daughter of Thomas de Scales, seventh Baron Scales, who died in 1460. He had no male heirs to succeed him, so his title passed on to his daughter Elizabeth, the first wife of Anthony Woodville, Elizabeth of York's maternal uncle. The fact that Kateryn did not inherit her father's title may point to the possibility that she was born out of wedlock. Although her name does not

32

"Of gentle birth and beautiful"

appear in the list of Elizabeth of York's ladies in 1502, she was important enough to have her own lodgings at court; that year, Henry VII paid "for the burying of a man that was slain in my Lady Grey's chamber".[24] Unfortunately, the circumstances of this man's mysterious death remain unknown.

Elizabeth of York's court seems to have been a byword for chastity, as her ladies-in-waiting were not embroiled in major scandals. The only scandal that involved one of the Queen's ladies occurred at some point in 1503 when Charles Brandon, a young man who served at the royal table, entered into a pre-contract with Elizabeth of York's maid of honour, Anne Browne. Anne was one of "the three gentlewomen of honour" who attended the Queen; other ladies who served in this capacity were Margaret Wotton and Anne Green.[25] The Queen's privy purse expenses for the year 1503 show that Anne Browne and Margaret Wotton received their wages for "half a year ended at Michaelmas last passed".[26] Charles Brandon's father, William, was Henry VII's standard bearer during the Battle of Bosworth in 1485; he was slain by Richard III. Charles was subsequently given a post of honour at court, serving at the King's table. Serving at court, he fell in love with Anne Browne and "resorted much" to her company.[27] Anne reciprocated his feelings and agreed to marry him. The couple entered into a pre-contract, which, if consummated, was as binding as marriage. Anne and Charles consummated their

Great Ladies

relationship, and Anne soon became pregnant; she gave birth to her first child, a daughter also named Anne, before the solemnization of marriage. But Charles was not fully committed to Anne and soon abandoned her to marry her aunt, Margaret Mortimer, who was some twenty years his senior and a very rich woman. Breaking one's promise was seen as dishonourable, and Anne Browne soon made it clear that Charles Brandon was pre-contracted to her and their match was consummated, making their relationship indissoluble. Brandon's marriage to Margaret Mortimer was soon annulled, and he married Anne Browne at some point during the early reign of Henry VIII.

On 2 February 1503, the feast of Candlemas, Elizabeth of York went into premature labour at the Tower of London. She died on 11 February, on the thirty-seventh anniversary of her birth. The Queen's daughter was named Katherine, but she did not survive for long and soon followed her mother to the grave. The Queen was sincerely mourned by her subjects and was given an elaborate and costly funeral. Her ladies-in-waiting and maids of honour took part in the obsequies, performing their last duty towards their deceased royal mistress. Elizabeth of York was outlived by four of her sisters: Cecily, Anne, Katherine and Bridget. The longest living of them all was Katherine, who married William Courtenay, Earl of Devon. The Queen's death was a huge blow to Katharine of

"Of gentle birth and beautiful"

Aragon, who had formed a close relationship with her. Henry VII briefly toyed with the idea of marrying Katharine after his wife's death, but the suggestion enraged Isabella of Castile, who said that "merely to have spoken of it is offensive to the ears, and we will not agree to it for anything in the world".[28] Henry VII was eager to maintain the Anglo-Spanish alliance and agreed to a marriage between Katharine and his younger son, Henry, heir to the throne.

Katharine's dowry was not yet paid, and the King now had to provide for her royal household. This proved harder than Henry VII had initially thought because Katharine's servants were unable to "live in peace with one another", and the young Dowager Princess of Wales was so liberal in spending money that Dona Elvira Manuel had to keep a tighter rein over her expenditures.[29] By 1505, Katharine of Aragon's circumstances had changed dramatically for the worse. Isabella of Castile's death on 26 November 1504 devalued Katharine's position in the marriage market and, subsequently, at the Tudor court. As a daughter of the widowed King of Aragon, who failed to pay the second instalment of her marriage portion, she was not such a prestigious match anymore, and on 27 June 1505, Henry, Prince of Wales, renounced his betrothal to her. Katharine's devastation was further increased when Dona Elvira, whose health was deteriorating by now, had to leave for Flanders for an eye operation. Katharine wrote to Ferdinand:

"Now, my Lord, a few days ago Dona Elvira de Manuel asked my leave to go to Flanders to get cured of a complaint which has come into her eyes, so that she lost the sight of one of them; and there is a physician in Flanders who cured the Infanta Isabel of the same disease with which she is afflicted. She laboured to bring him here so as not to leave me, but could never succeed with him; and I, since if she were blind she could not serve me, durst not hinder her journey."[30]

Katharine was not entirely honest with her father. She failed to mention that Dona Elvira betrayed her trust by conspiring against Katharine's father and had to be sent away; an eye operation was merely an excuse. Whatever the circumstances of Elvira's departure, the truth was that Katharine lost her chief lady of honour, whose betrayal shook her to the core and helped her realise that ladies-in-waiting had their own political agendas. Elvira was a forceful personality who imposed strict rules on Katharine, but she was a precious link to Katharine's childhood. Katharine now wanted a new lady of honour to superintend her household:

"I begged the King of England, my Lord, that until our Dona Elvira should return, his Highness would command that

"Of gentle birth and beautiful"

I should have, as a companion, an old English lady, or that he would take me to his court . . ."[31]

Henry VII decided to use this opportunity and dissolve Katharine's expensive Spanish household, absorbing it into his own. She was no longer "mistress of it" and lost her own independence. It was a huge blow for Katharine, who blamed the Spanish ambassador Rodrigo de Puebla and demanded his recall from England. Katharine's financial situation was now worse than ever. Without the dowry money, she was left destitute and had to pawn jewels, plate and ornaments she brought with her from Spain in 1501. A tone of bitter resentment now crept into her letters addressed to Ferdinand of Aragon. She reminded him that she had written many times to him, "supplicating you to order a remedy for my extreme necessity". Now she was bolder because she had run up debts in London and had no money to pay her servants' wages:

"I am in the greatest trouble and anguish in the world. On the one part, seeing all my people that they are ready to ask alms; on the other, the debts which I have in London; on the other, about my own person, I have nothing for chemises; wherefore, by your Highness's life, I have now sold some bracelets to get a dress of black velvet, for I was all but naked: for since I departed thence (from Spain) I have nothing except two new dresses, for till now those I brought from thence have lasted me; although now I have nothing but the dresses of brocade. On this account I supplicate your Highness to command to remedy this, and that as quickly as may be; for certainly I shall not be able to live in this manner."[32]

The most embarrassing part of being destitute was being unable to reward her loyal Spanish servants. In the sixteenth century, there existed a strong bond between royals and members of their households. Servants accompanied royalty on a daily basis, and deep bonds of loyalty, friendship, trust and mutual respect were easily forged in such circumstances. Households were often referred to as extended families in documents, and providing for one's servants was considered one of the greatest responsibilities of royal persons. Katharine felt such an obligation towards her servants and especially the six damsels who came with her from Spain. They were young and still unmarried; they reasonably hoped to contract great marriages with members of English aristocracy, but Katharine of Aragon's own difficult situation influenced their marital prospects. In a series of letters to her father, Katharine broached the subject of suitable marriage portions for her maids. Some of them, like Maria de Salazar, had relatives abroad who selected suitable matches for them. Katharine implored Ferdinand:

"It is known to your Highness how Dona Maria de Salazar was lady to the Queen my mother, who is in blessed glory, and how her Highness sent her to come with me; and in

"Of gentle birth and beautiful"

addition to the service which she did to her Highness, she had served me well, and in all this has done as a worthy woman. Wherefore I supplicate your Highness that, as well on account of the one service as the other, you would command her to be paid, since I have nothing wherewith to pay her, and also because her sister, the wife of Monsieur d'Aymeria, has in view for her a marriage in Flanders, of which she cannot avail herself, nor hope that it can be accomplished, without knowing what the said Dona Maria has for a marriage portion."[33]

Ferdinand remained deaf to his daughter's pleas, but Katharine was determined to provide dowries for her ladies. In another letter, she again invoked the memory of her late mother, hoping that Ferdinand would help her for the sake of Isabella of Castile:

"Your Highness knoweth that there came hither with me six ladies, the which have served me right well and with much necessity, without I giving them one maravedi. Some of them were with the Queen my Lady (who have the holy joy), and they served her a long time: and for that it is reason that they should marry, and I have nothing for to give to them and to help them, I beseech your Highness for to do me a grace, and that you will command to give unto their marriages, and that you will please for to write unto me the sum that your Grace shall be pleased and served for to give them, for that I may make answer unto them that shall move of marriages unto them."[34]

Ferdinand failed to provide money, disappointing Katharine once more. Some of her ladies disappointed her as well. The beautiful and determined Francesca de Caceres deserted Katharine to marry a wealthy Genoese banker, Francisco Grimaldi. The way Katharine later spoke about Francesca proves that this betrayal broke her heart. Francesca had, in Katharine's words, "cast herself away", and Katharine made sure to let everyone know that Francesca did not deserve to be lady-in-waiting to a great royal lady. When many years later Francesca required a letter of recommendation before entering the service of Archduchess Margaret of Savoy in the Netherlands, Katharine replied that Francesca was "so perilous a woman that it shall be dangerous to put her in a strange house". She was not suitable in the household of another princess and should be sent "home into her country".[35]

Francesca was not the only lady who left Katharine's service before 1509. Maria de Rojas, who slept in Katharine's bed after Prince Arthur's death and became her royal mistress's confidante, married Don Alvaro de Mendoza at some point before Katharine became Queen in 1509 and moved to southern Spain. Katharine's reaction was not recorded, but she may have encouraged Maria to marry and

"Of gentle birth and beautiful"

leave England. Maria had already proved her loyalty to Katharine when, in late 1504, she accepted a wealthy English heir as her suitor, hoping to stay in Katharine's service. This suitor was Thomas Stanley, the grandson of Henry VII's stepfather and "the best match in the kingdom".[36] By August 1505, Maria had changed her mind and, pressured by Dona Elvira, accepted the proposal of Elvira's son. Maria never married him, leaving England—and Katharine—behind.

Henry VII, Katharine of Aragon's father-in-law, who caused her so much pain and annoyance, died on 21 April 1509. The seventeen-year-old Henry, Prince of Wales, was almost immediately declared King of England. Within two months, Katharine of Aragon became his wife and queen.

NOTES

[1] *Calendar of State Papers, Spain,* Volume 1, n. 21.
[2] *Calendar of State Papers, Venice,* Volume 1, n. 760.
[3] Ann Wroe, *Perkin: The Story of Deception,* p. 128.
[4] Ibid., p. 518.
[5] Ibid., pp. 375-78.
[6] Ibid.
[7] *The Chronicle of Iohn Hardyng,* (ed. Henry Ellis), p. 581.
[8] Francis Bacon, *The Works of Lord Bacon: With an Introductory Essay,* Volume 1, p. 779.
[9] *Calendar of State Papers, Venice,* Volume 5, n. 575.
[10] Reginald Pole, *Pole's Defence of the Unity of the Church,* p. 197.
[11] Francis Bacon, *The Works of Lord Bacon: With an Introductory Essay,* Volume 1, p. 782.
[12] *Calendar of State Papers, Spain,* Volume 1, n. 249.
[13] Ibid., n. 268.
[14] Ibid.

Great Ladies

[15] Patrick Williams, *Katharine of Aragon*, p. 103.

[16] *Calendar of State Papers, Spain,* Volume 1, n. 288.

[17] Read more in Chapter 3.

[18] *Calendar of State Papers, Venice,* Volume 5, n. 575.

[19] Alison Weir, *Elizabeth of York*, p. 372.

[20] *Calendar of State Papers, Spain,* Volume 1, n. 327.

[21] Ibid.

[22] Sir Nicholas Harris Nicolas, *Privy Purse Expenses of Elizabeth of York*, p. 62.

[23] Caroline Metcalfe, *History: The Mystery of Dame Katherine Grey* [http://www.eastgrinsteadonline.com/2015/04/26/history-the-mystery-of-dame-katherine-grey/]

[24] Sir Nicholas Harris Nicolas, *Privy Purse Expenses of Elizabeth of York*, p. 182.

[25] David Starkey, *Rivals in Power*, p. 40.

[26] Sir Nicholas Harris Nicolas, *Privy Purse Expenses of Elizabeth of York*, p. 99.

[27] David Starkey, op.cit.

[28] *Calendar of State Papers, Spain,* Volume 1, n. 360.

[29] Ibid., n. 400, 401.

[30] M.A. Everett Wood, *Letters of Royal and Illustrious Ladies of Great Britain*, Volume 1, p. 132.

[31] Ibid.

[32] Ibid., pp. 138-40.

[33] Ibid., p. 126.

[34] Ibid., pp. 129-30.

[35] *Letters and Papers, Foreign and Domestic, Henry VIII,* Volume 1, n. 2120.

[36] *Calendar of State Papers, Spain,* Volume 1, n. 420.

CHAPTER 3
"THE DAMSELS OF HER COURT"

Henry VIII was determined to marry Katharine of Aragon, even though the most influential people at court advised him not to. His councillors and grandmother, Margaret Beaufort, pressed him to forget about the Spanish infanta and marry the French King's sister.[1] But Henry was infatuated and impatient. In a letter to Katharine's former sister-in-law, Archduchess Margaret of Savoy, the young King wrote that "even if we were still free, it is she, nevertheless, that we would choose for our wife before all other".[2] The fact that Katharine used to be his late brother's wife did not bother Henry much, or at least not yet. Although six years older than him—she was twenty-three to his seventeen—Katharine was young, beautiful and fun-loving. In the words of up-and-coming courtier Thomas More, Katharine possessed "all those qualities that make for beauty in a very charming young girl"; Henry clearly agreed because he wanted no other bride but her.[3]

The couple married in a private ceremony in a chapel at Greenwich Palace on 11 June 1509. Thirteen days later, they

Great Ladies

were jointly crowned in Westminster Abbey. Among the Spanish ladies who witnessed Katharine of Aragon's triumph were Maria de Salinas and Ines (known in England as Agnes) de Venegas. By 30 July 1509, Agnes de Venegas was married to William Blount, Baron Mountjoy, who must have been courting her before Katharine of Aragon's coronation. Because the King held William Blount in "high esteem", he wrote to Ferdinand of Aragon requesting him to grant the legacy which Queen Isabella of Castile had left Agnes and to restore some of her property.[4]

Maria de Salinas also had a bright future ahead of her. In 1516, Maria, "who has faithfully served her [Katharine of Aragon], and who has always comforted her in her hours of trial", received letters patent of denization and married William Willoughby, Baron Willoughby de Eresby.[5] Katharine of Aragon and Henry VIII financed Lady Willoughby's marriage, giving her a dowry worth eleven hundred marks. She was so much favoured by Katharine that it was said that the Queen loved her "more than any other mortal".[6] Henry VIII was also fond of her and named one of his warships after her. The Queen recompensed Maria for sticking with her during her penurious widowhood and often presented her with expensive gifts, such as a golden cup and spoons—objects so precious that Maria's husband mentioned them in his last will.[7]

"The damsels of her court"

On 29 July 1509, most of the members of Katharine of Aragon's Spanish household left England. In a letter to her father, Katharine wrote: "My mistress, Janina de Cuero, my chamberlain, with my other servants, set off from hence to their homes."[8] She now had her new household—that of an English Queen consort—formed. Some Spaniards retained their posts, but they were in the minority. Katharine now had to befriend English ladies, who eagerly sought employment in the Queen's household. Still, when she prematurely gave birth to a daughter on 31 January 1510, there were no English ladies-in-waiting in attendance. The Queen's Spanish confessor, Fray Diego Fernandez, reported that "this affair was so secret that no one knew it until now, except the King my Lord, two Spanish women, a physician and I".[9] These two Spanish women were, presumably, Agnes de Venegas and Maria de Salinas.

The young Queen quickly made new friends. One of them was Elizabeth Stafford, Queen Elizabeth of York's much favoured first cousin and chief lady-in-waiting. In 1505, she married Robert Radcliffe, Lord FitzWalter, and was thus known at court as Lady FitzWalter. She had a younger sister named Anne, who was married to George Hastings, Earl of Huntingdon. Elizabeth, who was the Queen's new favourite attendant, soon noticed that Henry VIII was having clandestine meetings with her sister. William Compton, one of the King's friends and his Groom of the Stool, helped to arrange these trysts with Anne Hastings, who became Henry's first recorded royal mistress. The Spanish ambassador Luis Caroz reported that Lady FitzWalter, being anxious for her sister's well-being, conferred with her brother, Edward Stafford, third Duke of Buckingham, her husband and her sister's husband. The end result was that the proud Buckingham argued with William Compton and reproached him "in many and very hard words". The King was "so offended at this that he reprimanded the Duke angrily". The whole affair ended in the most sordid scandal of the early reign of Henry VIII. Buckingham left court in a huff, George Hastings placed his unfaithful wife in a convent and the King banished Lady FitzWalter and her husband.

The young King did not like that his wife's ladies-in-waiting were "insidiously spying out every unwatched moment in order to tell the Queen", and he wanted to banish many more whom he believed were conspiring with Lady FitzWalter, but he thought it would cause "too great a scandal". The damage was already done, however. The whole court knew that "the Queen had been vexed with the King and the King with her" and that "this storm went on between them".[10] Katharine of Aragon manifested her annoyance very publicly and shut herself away in her private apartments. The reason Lady FitzWalter spied on her sister and told the Queen

"The damsels of her court"

about Anne's secret affair with Henry VIII is that the ladies-in-waiting were not used to witnessing scandals like this during the previous reign. Henry VII had no recorded mistresses while Elizabeth of York was alive, and everyone assumed that Henry VIII would follow into his father's footsteps and be a faithful husband. Henry, however, had other ideas. By 1515, his reputation as a womaniser was already well established. "The King is a youngling", wrote the French ambassador, "who cares for nothing but girls and hunting, and wastes his father's patrimony".[11]

Between 1510 and 1518, Katharine of Aragon experienced six pregnancies, but only one of them ended successfully, and her child, a daughter Mary, lived past infancy. The contrast between the worn-out Queen and her young, vivacious ladies-in-waiting soon became noticeable. In 1514, the Venetian ambassador described the Queen as "rather ugly than otherwise" but praised "the damsels of her court" as "handsome" and of "sumptuous appearance".[12] These ladies often made great impressions on ambassadors, who admired not only their beauty but also their language skills and apparel. In 1518, it was noticed that "lady maskers" spoke "good French" with the French ambassadors, "which delighted these gentlemen, to hear these ladies speak to them in their own tongue". Nine years later, the Venetian ambassador admired "the ladies, whose various styles of beauty and apparel, enhanced by the brilliancy of the lights, caused me to think I was contemplating the choirs of angels". These "angels" and "goddesses rather than human beings" were the leading luminaries of Henry VIII's court. Naturally, the King selected his mistresses from among these young and charming damsels, but beauty was not the only factor in choosing a partner.[13]

Henry, who dabbled in composing music and poetry, paid much attention to women with similar skills. One of his wife's maids of honour, Elizabeth "Bessie" Blount, caught his eye because she was an excellent singer and dancer. Chronicler Edward Hall recorded that "the King in his fresh youth was in the chains of love with a fair damsel called Elizabeth Blount, daughter of Sir John Blount, knight; which damsel, in singing, dancing, and in all goodly pastimes, exceeded all other; by which goodly pastimes she won the King's heart".[14] The reason why Henry's love affair with Bessie was recorded in a chronicle of the reign is because, on 18 June 1519, she gave birth to Henry VIII's illegitimate son, Henry FitzRoy. Bessie was unmarried at the time of her son's birth, and the King acknowledged the boy as his own. Hall called FitzRoy "a goodly man child, of beauty like to the father and mother".[15]

When exactly the King's infatuation with Bessie started remains unclear. She was listed among the Queen's ladies for

"The damsels of her court"

her "year's wages" in May 1513; a year later, she appeared as one of the "persons in the mummery" on Christmas Day.[16] Her marriage to Gilbert Tailboys, contracted at some point in 1522, is usually interpreted as the end of her relationship with Henry VIII. That Henry VIII ordered Cardinal Thomas Wolsey, his chief advisor, to find Bessie a suitable husband is confirmed by charges against the Cardinal in 1530. Wolsey was blamed for encouraging "the young gentlewomen of the realm to be . . . concubines by the well marrying of Bessie Blount".[17]

Despite the very public outburst of jealousy at her husband's first extramarital affair, Katharine of Aragon soon found a way to "shut her eyes and endure" Henry VIII's numerous liaisons.[18] She sought solace in motherhood and religion. In 1516, she gave birth to Princess Mary, whom she groomed to become Queen. Henry was uneasy about accepting a girl as his heiress. On 18 June 1525, he raised his illegitimate son's social status by creating him Duke of Richmond and Somerset. It was a painful blow to Katharine of Aragon. The perceptive Venetian ambassador recorded: "It seems that the Queen resents the earldom and dukedom conferred on the King's natural son and remains dissatisfied, at the instigation, it is said, of three of her Spanish ladies, her chief counsellors, so the King has dismissed them from the court—a strong measure, but the Queen was obliged to submit and to have

49

Great Ladies

patience".[19] Considering the Spanish ladies-in-waiting's background, it does not seem one bit surprising that they instigated the Queen's dissatisfaction. Katharine was the daughter of Isabella of Castile, who ruled over Spain with an iron fist and became a legend during her own lifetime. A woman could and did rule in her own right, it seemed obvious to Katharine and her compatriots. But it looked different in England. In 1533, the imperial ambassador was to remark that Henry VIII "received the principal title to his realm through the female line".[20] Henry knew that his mother's claim to the throne was bypassed, and she was only queen consort, although she could have been queen regnant like Isabella in Spain. The birth of Henry FitzRoy in 1519 ensured the King that the lack of male heirs was not his fault, but he was still married to Katharine of Aragon, whose last recorded pregnancy ended with the birth of a stillborn daughter on 9 November 1518.

On 22 June 1527, Henry VIII informed Katharine of Aragon that he wished to annul their marriage because his conscience troubled him. It was now that the King began to think that God was punishing him with the lack of male heirs for marrying his brother's widow. In the biblical book of Leviticus, God warned against such relationships: "Thou shalt not uncover the nakedness of thy brother's wife: it is thy brother's nakedness", and again, "If a man shall take his

"The damsels of her court"

brother's wife, it is an impurity: he hath uncovered his brother's nakedness; they shall be childless".[21] By September, the Queen knew that her husband had had an affair with one of her maids of honour. Katharine was used to her husband's philandering ways, but he now wanted to marry the lady who refused to become his mistress, and to this the Queen could not agree. This lady was Anne Boleyn, daughter and niece to the Boleyn women who had served as Katharine of Aragon's ladies-in-waiting since 1509.

Anne Boleyn joined the ranks of Katharine of Aragon's maids of honour in 1522. The erudite and well-educated twenty-two-year-old Anne first served as Archduchess Margaret of Savoy's demoiselle and then transferred to the household of Henry VIII's younger sister, Mary Tudor, who married King Louis XII of France in 1514. After Louis's death in early 1515, Mary and her entourage left France, but Anne was retained by the new French Queen, Claude, and remained in her service for seven years. Upon her return, Anne was said to have been very French in the way of dressing and manners. Like most fashionable women at court, she favoured the French style of dressing, wearing shapely headdresses revealing a generous amount of hair and low-cut, figure-hugging gowns with large sleeves. Anne's mother, Elizabeth Boleyn, was a daughter of Thomas Howard, second Duke of Norfolk, and Anne prided herself on her descent from this

Great Ladies

branch of the Howard line. Her father, Sir Thomas Boleyn, was a seasoned courtier and diplomat who served as an ambassador; his embassy to the court of Margaret of Savoy in 1512 gave him the opportunity to place Anne in the archduchess's household.

Anne had many talents. One contemporary observed that "she knew how to sing and dance well" and played on a lute. In "behaviour, manners, attire and tongue" she was said to have excelled other ladies at court.[22] She also had a unique type of beauty: with olive skin, dark hair and a willowy figure, she looked different than most pale and plump English roses. At some point in 1526, Henry VIII noticed Anne and began his courtship of her. Her elder sister, Mary Carey, was his mistress, and the infatuated King assumed that Anne would also succumb to his charm. But Anne knew that virginity was much prized in a woman and prospective wife, and she aimed to marry well. Only recently she had been hotly pursued by Henry Percy, the heir of the Earl of Northumberland. In an epistle to her father, she had once mused: "I understand from your letter that you desire me to be a woman of good reputation when I come to court".[23] She intended to defend her good reputation and refused to become Henry VIII's mistress. Anne's refusal shocked the King, but he was intrigued at the same time. No other lady had ever said such a firm "no" to his advances.

"The damsels of her court"

Anne withdrew from court, but Henry kept sending letter after letter to the woman who soon became his obsession. The son of Margaret Pole, Reginald, would later claim that Anne sent her chaplains, "grave theologians", to convince the King to set his wife aside because she was his brother's widow and their marriage was thus illegal in the eyes of God.[24] Although he was a hostile witness, Reginald's claim cannot be dismissed lightly because he assisted the King during the early stages of the divorce case before deciding to leave England in 1532. Anne herself later boasted that Henry was bound to her "for she extricated him from a state of sin".[25] Henry VIII had once mused that he would not be able to marry Katharine of Aragon because she was his late brother's widow, and now he was eager to prove that Prince Arthur knew Katharine carnally.

The King argued that he was sinfully—and thus illegally—married to Katharine of Aragon because she had carnally known his brother. Henry VIII's whole argument hinged on Katharine's first marriage being consummated and her not being a virgin when she married him in 1509. But Katharine defied him. She had spent only seven nights with Arthur and had emerged from this marriage "as intact and undefiled as she had come from her mother's womb".[26] The clerics and lawyers who worked to extricate Henry from his marriage agreed that "these were the worst points [against the

Great Ladies

divorce] that could be imagined".[27] These points were "the worst" because they were difficult to prove or disprove, and the only person who knew the truth was Katharine herself.

In 1529, the divorce proceedings reached the point of a public trial that took place in the parliament chamber of the Dominican friary in London known as Blackfriars. The Queen appeared in person on 18 June 1529 with "a great company of ladies and gentlewomen following her". She threw herself on her knees and addressed Henry VIII in loud, broken English, affirming that when he first had her, she was "a true maid without touch of man; and whether it be true or no, I put it to your conscience".[28] She left the court never to return again, but the proceedings went on without her. "If the matter was to be decided by women", mused the French ambassador, the King "would lose the battle". The women who gathered at court that day "did not fail to encourage the Queen at her entrance and departure by their cries, telling her to care for nothing". Katharine "recommended herself to their good prayers" and resorted "to other Spanish tricks".[29] The King was speechless at his wife's bravado and the overwhelming support of women, but he decided to put Katharine's virginity on trial, humiliating her in the process.

Starting on 28 June 1529, a series of depositions was made concerning the witnesses to the Queen's first marriage. Amongst them were ladies-in-waiting who were now

"The damsels of her court"

advanced in years, but who in 1501 were young women. Jane Guildford, née Vaux, was a seasoned lady-in-waiting. Born in 1469, she served as a maid of honour to Elizabeth of York and later as a lady-in-waiting to Margaret Beaufort and was present during Katharine of Aragon's marriage to Prince Arthur in St Paul's Cathedral in 1501. Jane was half-French; her mother, Katherine Vaux, née Peniston, was a daughter of an English exile living in Provence. Katherine served as a lady-in-waiting to Margaret of Anjou, wife of Henry VI, and followed her royal mistress to exile in 1476. She returned to England after Margaret died in 1482; she appeared as one of Elizabeth of York's ladies as "Dame Katheryn Vaux" during the Queen's coronation in 1487.[30] Following into her mother's footsteps, Jane showed fierce loyalty to the royal women she served. She first became lady governess to Henry VII's daughters, Margaret and Mary, and impressed the scholar Erasmus, who visited the royal nursery at Eltham Palace in 1497. Many years later, in a letter to Jane's son, Sir Henry Guildford, Erasmus sent his "warmest good wishes to the noble lady, your mother, whose acquaintance I owe to several conversations".[31]

Jane's excellent knowledge of the French language and her impeccable manners earned her a spot among the ladies who followed Mary Tudor to France in October 1514. Mary was very fond of "my Mother Guildford", as she affectionately called Jane. She was devastated when Louis XII sent Mother Guildford home soon after the wedding. The reason Jane was recalled was that Louis XII believed she exerted too much influence on Mary. Mary admitted as much herself when she wrote that after Jane's departure she was left with "such [ladies] as never had experience or knowledge how to . . . give me counsel in time of need". Louis believed that without her chief lady-in-waiting, who was also her mother figure, Mary would more easily adjust to life at the French court. It seems that Jane Guildford insisted that her royal charge spoke to other people only in her presence; she was also eager to accompany Mary to the bedchamber she shared with Louis—or at least this is what the French King told the English envoys.[32] Jane never returned to Mary Tudor's French household, but the young Queen returned to England in May 1515 after Louis XII died unexpectedly in January.

Jane Guildford continued her royal service and became an influential member of the court. Her son Henry and brother Nicholas were indispensable servants and personal favourites of Henry VIII's. By 1529, the sixty-year-old Lady Guildford was believed to have possessed knowledge concerning Katharine of Aragon's virginity. From among three senior ladies of the court, it was Jane's testimony that proved to have been the most detailed and, potentially, the most damning to the Queen's case. She deposed that she saw Prince Arthur and

"The damsels of her court"

Katharine of Aragon on their wedding night "lying in bed together alone and sole and in mind and intent as she believeth to have carnal cognition together as man and wife". She left them in their bedchamber for the night and returned the next morning "as her office required" and saw them again "in bed sole, likewise as she did leave them the night before".[33] Jane also deposed that she heard Elizabeth of York, Henry VII and Prince Arthur saying that "the said Prince Arthur and Lady Katharine lay together in bed as man and wife all alone five or six nights after the said marriage".[34] This, in essence, was what happened. Katharine herself later claimed that she and Arthur slept in one bed together seven nights but never had sex.

Another lady who was with Katharine and Arthur that night was Agnes Howard, née Tilney, Dowager Duchess of Norfolk and step-grandmother of Henry VIII's wife-to-be. Born in 1477, she "knew Henry VII and his Queen Elizabeth from the time she was fifteen" and remembered Katharine of Aragon's arrival from Spain. The night after their wedding, Agnes deposed, she saw Arthur and Katharine "lying in one bed . . . and left them so lying together there the said night".[35]

Another lady who was present was Mary Bourchier, née Say, Countess of Essex. She was the same age as the Queen and deposed that "Prince Arthur and Katharine lived as man and wife together; that the two occupied the same bed after the wedding, at London House, and were generally reputed as man and wife".[36] This was what happened in 1501 as seen through the eyes of ladies-in-waiting who accompanied the young couple. But these depositions proved nothing; Katharine of Aragon herself claimed to have slept with Arthur in one bed during seven nights and emerge from it a virgin.

Surprisingly, several men who were interrogated revealed much more than the three abovementioned women. Thomas Grey, second Marquis of Dorset, said that he was present when Prince Arthur went to bed after his wedding and saw Katharine lying "under the coverlet, as the manner is of queens in that behalf". Dorset believed that Arthur and Katharine cohabited because the prince was "of a good and sanguine complexion, and they were commonly reputed as man and wife during Prince Arthur's life".[37] Anthony Willoughby, who served Arthur for five years, said that he saw the prince retiring to bed with Katharine after their wedding. The next morning, Arthur emerged from his bedchamber boasting that "it is good pastime to have a wife" and calling for a cup of ale because he had been "this night in the midst of Spain".[38] The insinuation was clear: Arthur knew Katharine carnally.

Whereas the English courtiers portrayed Arthur as a boisterous youngling, the Spanish depicted him as weak and frail. In 1531, at a hearing in Zaragoza, Spain, Katharine of

"The damsels of her court"

Aragon's former attendants testified that Francesca de Caceres, who was one of Katharine's favourites, "was looking sad and telling the other ladies that nothing had passed between Prince Arthur and his wife".[39] Another witness, Dr Alcaraz, testified that Arthur's "limbs were weak and that he had never seen a man whose legs and other bits of his body were so thin".[40] This statement was corroborated by the Spanish ambassador Fuensalida, who wrote in 1501 that Henry VII made a decision that Arthur "will know his wife sexually on the day of the wedding and then separate himself from her for two or three years because it is said that the prince is frail, and the King . . . wanted to have them [Arthur and Katharine of Aragon] with him for the first three years [of their marriage] so that the prince should mature in strength".[41] These requirements were grounded in concern for Arthur because a surfeit of sexual activity at an early age was believed to lead to an early death.

Whether Arthur and Katharine knew each other carnally will never be known for a fact, but the Queen would maintain until her dying day that they never consummated their short-lived marriage.

NOTES

[1] *Calendar of State Papers, Spain,* Volume 4 Part 1, Henry VIII, n. 572.
[2] *Letters and Papers, Foreign and Domestic, Henry VIII,* Volume 1, n. 119.

Great Ladies

[3] Giles Tremlett, *Catherine of Aragon: Henry's Spanish Queen*, p. 83.

[4] *Calendar of State Papers, Spain,* Volume 2, n. 20.

[5] Ibid., n. 238.

[6] Ibid., n. 201.

[7] "I bequeath to my said wife a cup of gold and two spoons of gold and a salt of gold that the Queen gave to her". PROB 11/23, ff. 227-9

[8] M.A. Everett Wood, *Letters of Royal and Illustrious Ladies of Great Britain,* Volume 1, p. 160.

[9] *Calendar of State Papers, Spain,* Supplement To Volumes 1 and 2, n. 7.

[10] Ibid., n. 8.

[11] *Letters and Papers, Foreign and Domestic, Henry VIII,* Volume 2, n. 1105.

[12] Sebastiano Giustiniani, *Four Years at the Court of Henry VIII,* Volume 1, p. 81.

[13] Sylvia Barbara Soberton, *Golden Age Ladies,* p. 65.

[14] Edward Hall, *Hall's Chronicle,* p. 703.

[15] Ibid.

[16] *Letters and Papers, Foreign and Domestic, Henry VIII,* Volume 4, p. cxlv.

[17] Ibid.

[18] *Letters and Papers, Foreign and Domestic, Henry VIII,* Volume 6, n. 1069.

[19] *Calendar of State Papers, Venice,* Volume 3, n. 1053.

[20] *Letters and Papers, Foreign and Domestic, Henry VIII,* Volume 6, n. 351.

[21] J. J. Scarisbrick, *Henry VIII,* p. 163.

[22] Eric Ives, *The Life and Death of Anne Boleyn,* p. 45.

[23] Ibid., p.19.

[24] Reginald Pole, *Defence of the Unity of the Church,* pp. 181-85.

[25] *Letters and Papers, Foreign and Domestic, Henry VIII,* Volume 8, n. 666.

[26] *Calendar of State Papers, Spain,* Volume 3 Part 2, n. 550.

[27] *State Papers,* Volume 1, p. 195.

[28] George Cavendish, *The Life of Cardinal Wolsey,* Volume 1, p. 150.

[29] *Letters and Papers, Foreign and Domestic, Henry VIII,* Volume 4, n. 5702.

[30] John Leland, *Collectanea,* pp. 206, 229, 233.

[31] Peter G. Bietenholz, *The Correspondence of Erasmus: Letters 842-992 (1518-1519),* p. 365.

[32] M.A. Everett Green, *Lives of the Princesses of England: From the Norman Conquest,* Volume 5, pp. 47-9.

"The damsels of her court"

[33] PRO SP 1/65, f. 19r quoted by Godfrey Anstruther, *Vaux of Harrowden: A Recusant Family*, p. 13.
[34] Ibid.
[35] *Letters and Papers, Foreign and Domestic, Henry VIII*, Volume 4, n. 5778.
[36] Ibid.
[37] Ibid., n. 5774.
[38] Ibid., n. 5773.
[39] Real Academia de Historia MS. 9-4674, quoted by Giles Tremlett, *Catherine of Aragon*, p. 89.
[40] Ibid., p. 99.
[41] Patrick Williams, *Katharine of Aragon*, p. 101.

CHAPTER 4
"I AM A WOMAN"

In the summer of 1531, Henry VIII exiled Katharine of Aragon, sending her to the More, a former residence of Cardinal Wolsey. As she was still his wife and Queen of England, Katharine retained a large household. A Venetian visitor who saw the Queen dine in state on the morning of 25 August 1531 reported that her court consisted of two hundred members; she also had "some thirty maids of honour standing round the table and about fifty who performed its service".[1] Yet visits of foreign diplomats like this were rare, and the King had already started isolating Katharine in order to break her. Anne Boleyn also became bolder in her opposition to the Queen. She once shocked the Queen's ladies-in-waiting when she boasted that she would like to see all the Spaniards "at the bottom of the sea". When one of Katharine's ladies reproached Anne "for the sake of the Queen's honour", Anne insolently replied that she cared not for Katharine and "would rather see her hanged than have to confess that she was her Queen and mistress".[2] She also installed some of her trusted ladies in the Queen's service "to spy and report anything she may say or do".[3]

"I am a woman"

Anne Boleyn and a train of her ladies were a visible presence during the Christmas festivities of 1532. Anne was "accompanied by almost as many ladies as if she were Queen" and received a magnificent present from Henry VIII, whereas Katharine of Aragon and her women received nothing.[4] Yet, as one chronicler observed, "the men said that there was no mirth that Christmas because the Queen and the ladies were absent".[5] Whereas some people detested Anne Boleyn's influence and spread malicious rumours about her, others understood that her friendship was valuable and could bring benefits if Anne became Queen. One such person was Honor, Viscountess Lisle. Born as Honor Grenville c. 1493-95, Lady Lisle had seven children by her first husband, Sir John Basset, who died in 1528. Her second husband was Arthur Plantagenet, Viscount Lisle, the illegitimate son of King Edward IV. This marriage brought Honor greater social prominence, as illustrated by her growing network of friends and clients at court. In the summer of 1532, she began sending gifts to Anne and used one of her favourite servants, George Taylor, as an intermediary. Lady Lisle sent peewits for Anne's table, for which she gave her "great thanks", and an archer's bow that was "somewhat too big". In exchange for these and future presents, Lady Lisle asked for Anne's assistance in obtaining an import/export license. George Taylor wrote that Anne denied the request "for certain causes" but "she do trust to do you good some other ways, which she said she would gladly do as to anybody".[6]

In October 1532, Lady Lisle went to Calais with Anne Boleyn and some twenty other ladies-in-waiting. Earlier that autumn, Henry VIII had raised Anne to the peerage by creating her Marchioness of Pembroke in her own right. With her social status raised so high, Anne was eligible as Henry's future wife, and the King presented her to Francis I and his nobles. Anne and her ladies, dressed in robes dripping with gold, danced with the French gentlemen and dazzled the spectators. Anne was reportedly living like a Queen in Calais and ceremoniously accompanied the King to Mass and everywhere else. In early January 1533, Anne's ladies-in-waiting would have noticed that their mistress's waist was thickening and her stomach was rounded. It soon became apparent that she was expecting her first child. The King married Anne in great secret on 25 January 1533, with only a handful of servants in attendance. In February, both the King and Anne were in jovial moods. Anne hosted a lavish banquet in her private apartments with members of her family and entourage present. Henry VIII, who sat next to Anne's step-grandmother, Agnes Howard, Dowager Duchess of Norfolk, asked her if Anne, "the Marchioness", as he fondly referred to her, was not a wealthy lady who could bring her husband a large dowry? The King was dropping heavy hints that he was planning to marry his beloved lady.[7] In late

"I am a woman"

March, the Imperial ambassador reported that "the Lady's royal household" was already appointed, and on 12 April, Anne was ceremoniously led to Mass as Queen of England, accompanied by sixty maids of honour.[8] On 1 June 1533, she was solemnly crowned in Westminster Abbey. Anne Boleyn's coronation divided the courtiers. A tight group consisting mostly of her family and friends clustered around the new Queen, whereas others remained loyal to Katharine of Aragon and her daughter, Mary.

On 3 July 1533, a little over a month after Anne's coronation, Katharine was informed that she was no longer Queen of England, but Princess Dowager of Wales, a title she received after her first husband's death. Katharine refused to countenance this change and did not react when the King's officials referred to her by any other title than Queen. Many of her servants followed suit and refused to call her Princess Dowager, arguing that when they swore their oaths so many years ago, they "were sworn to King Henry and Queen Katharine". Maintaining two royal households was expensive, and Henry decided to reduce Katharine's establishment, cutting costs wherever possible.

On 7 September 1533, Anne Boleyn gave birth to a daughter. Henry VIII, who hoped to have a son and heir, was disappointed, but he had to move forward with his policies. The infant Elizabeth superseded Katharine of Aragon's

Great Ladies

daughter, Mary, in the line of succession. Her christening was a major political event used to shut down Anne's critics. The King invited the most prominent members of the nobility who were also Katharine of Aragon's supporters. Henry Courtenay, Marquess of Exeter—Henry VIII's first cousin—carried "a taper of virgin wax". Next to him was Henry Grey, Marquess of Dorset "bearing the salt". The godparents were Thomas Cranmer, Archbishop of Canterbury, Agnes Howard, Dowager Duchess of Norfolk, and Margaret Grey, Dowager Marchioness of Dorset. Immediately after the baptism, the little princess was confirmed with Gertrude Courtenay, Marchioness of Exeter, serving as an additional godmother.[9] The Dorsets and the Exeters were the cream of the English nobility, both families being closely related to Henry VIII. The Dorsets sprang from Elizabeth Woodville's first marriage to Sir John Grey, who was killed at the Battle of Towton in 1461. Henry Grey, third Marquess of Dorset, was Elizabeth Woodville's great-grandson. Henry Courtenay, Marquess of Exeter, was a son of Katherine of York and thus Henry VIII's first cousin.

Gertrude Courtenay, Marchioness of Exeter, was one of the closest associates of Katharine of Aragon. Anne Boleyn noticed that Gertrude was "most devoted to the Queen" and dismissed her from Katharine's service in 1530.[10] Gertrude was obliged to take part in Anne's coronation as one of the marchionesses who wore a demi-coronal of gold on her head.

"I am a woman"

When Gertrude was appointed as one of Princess Elizabeth's godmothers, rumours sprang at court that "she really wanted to have nothing to do with this" but took part "so as not to displease the King".[11] But Gertrude continued to displease Henry VIII and Anne Boleyn throughout Anne's time as Queen. In June 1533, she contacted Elizabeth Barton, the famous Nun of Kent, who was broadcasting anti-Boleyn prophecies. Barton had been known in court circles since 1528, and her prophetic visions were printed at about that time. Even the King himself had wondered whether her visions were genuine and ordered Sir Thomas More to investigate further. More was sceptical, but the King granted her an audience. Problems started when Barton began making political prophecies claiming, for instance, that if Henry VIII married Anne Boleyn, "then within one month after such marriage he should no longer be King of this realm, and in the reputation of Almighty God should not be a King one day nor one hour but would die a villain's death".[12] She also claimed that she saw in her visions a place reserved for the King in hell.

Gertrude Courtenay was aware that association with Barton was dangerous, so she travelled to see the nun in disguise. She swapped places with her servant, Constance Bontayn, who dressed as Gertrude in order to confuse anyone who might follow them. Gertrude and her husband had subsequently invited Barton to one of their properties at

Great Ladies

Horsley, where the nun fell into a trance. Barton's trances were as frightening as they were fascinating to the observers: "her face was wonderfully disfigured, her tongue hanging out, and her eyes being in a manner plucked out, and laid upon her cheeks, and so greatly distorted". There was also "a voice speaking within her belly, as it had been in a tun; her lips not greatly moving". Her voice was said to have been sweet and heavenly when she talked about "joys of heaven" and terrible when she spoke about hell.[13]

Elizabeth Barton and her accomplices—monks who helped her broadcast her prophecies—were arrested in the autumn of 1533. Under interrogation, Barton confessed that her prophecies were false. Gertrude Courtenay's involvement was soon discovered, and Barton was further interrogated about their association. The nun confessed that Gertrude sent two of her servants to take her to the marchioness's home at Horsley, but she exonerated Gertrude, saying that her motives were personal and had nothing to do with politics. "The chief cause why she sent for her", Barton said, was that she had borne children who lived not after their birth; and, supposing herself to be with child again, she desired Dame Elizabeth [Barton] to pray to Our Lady, that she might have issue that would live". Barton also told Gertrude that there would be war in England soon, and the marchioness "asked her to pray for her husband, that if he went over he might return safely".[14]

"I am a woman"

This exchange seemed innocent, but other interrogated witnesses reported that Gertrude and her husband were interested in Barton's prophecies concerning Henry VIII and his reign.[15] The King knew that Elizabeth Barton, who was very vocal in her support of Katharine of Aragon and wanted to obtain an audience with the former Queen, had become a figure of national importance. Henry never forgave her and sent Barton and five of her accomplices to the gallows on 20 April 1534.

Barton's execution sent a chilling message to everyone who opposed Henry VIII and his policies. Katharine of Aragon never granted the Nun of Kent the audience she craved, and now the former Queen was afraid that her friends and supporters would be executed. "She has no fear for herself", wrote the imperial ambassador Chapuys, "but she fears for the Marquess and Marchioness of Exeter, and the good Bishop of Rochester, who have been very familiar with" Elizabeth Barton.[16] Gertrude decided to write a pleading letter to Henry VIII. She acknowledged "mine abuse, lightness, and indiscreet offences committed as well as in frequenting the conversation and company of that most unworthy, subtle, and deceivable woman, called the Holy Maid of Kent". She succumbed to Barton's influence because, she said, "I am a woman, whose fragility and brittleness is such as most facilely, easily, and lightly is seduced and brought into abuse and light belief". She gave ear to Barton's "seditious tales" and "false prophecies" concerning the King, but she never harboured any malicious intentions against her sovereign.[17] Henry VIII forgave Gertrude, mostly because she was his first cousin's wife and thus a relative, but he kept a close eye on her and her family. In a letter to Thomas Cromwell, Gertrude wrote that the King's pardon was "much to my comfort", but she made an attempt to exonerate herself:

"I write to you as my Lord's very friend, that if the King speak of this matter you will answer for me that he has no more obedient subject; trusting he will remember that it is much less marvel that I, being a woman, shall be thus deluded by such pestilent hypocrites, seeing so many wise persons have been equally abused."[18]

Gertrude played her woman card well, referring to the misogynistic view that women were inferior to men in intellect and understanding and were easily manipulated. It is doubtful that she really held such beliefs, but she used them to her advantage and obtained pardon. But she would never stop supporting Katharine of Aragon and her daughter, Mary. By the time of Elizabeth Barton's execution, Mary had been degraded from the position of princess and became Lady Mary. A further blow came when her royal household was dissolved and she was forced to join the establishment of her younger half sister, Elizabeth.

"I am a woman"

Henry VIII broke with the Catholic Church and proclaimed himself the Supreme Head of the English Church. On 23 March 1534, parliament declared in the Act of Succession that Henry VIII's marriage to Anne Boleyn was lawful and that the succession to the throne was to devolve upon Anne's children. Mary thus became the King's illegitimate daughter, but she never accepted her new position. Anne Boleyn tried to reconcile Mary with her father if she only accepted her as Queen, but Mary refused, saying that "she knew no other Queen in England except her mother".[19] Anne was furious because she understood that her political enemies would cluster around this spirited teenager who insisted that she was the true princess of England. To gain more control over her unruly stepdaughter, Anne appointed her father's sister, Anne Shelton, as Lady Mistress of the joint household of Elizabeth and Mary.

Anne Shelton's appointment meant that Mary's governess, Margaret Pole, Countess of Salisbury, had to be dismissed. Margaret had formed a close bond with Katharine of Aragon and treated her daughter with the same warmth. She joined Mary's household when the princess was nine and instantly became a mother figure and a favourite. When Mary's household was dissolved in December 1533, Margaret "offered to follow and serve her at her own expense, with an honourable train of servants", but the King declined the

Great Ladies

offer.[20] Henry VIII never particularly liked Margaret, who was a powerful landowner and one of only two women in England who held an aristocratic title in her own right (the second being Anne Boleyn as Marchioness of Pembroke), and blamed her for setting Mary against him. The sixty-year-old Margaret left Mary's service in early 1534 and fell sick soon afterwards. On 12 February 1534, one of her sons, Henry Pole, Baron Montague, wrote to Honor Lisle: "My Lady my mother lies at Bisham, to whom I made your ladyship's recommendations. I assure you she is very weak, but it was to her great comfort to hear of my lord and your ladyship."[21]

Mary did not expect her new Lady Mistress to treat her with warm feelings because Anne Shelton's loyalty lay with her niece, Anne Boleyn, but even Shelton found her imperious niece's instructions to be too harsh. Whenever Mary used the title of princess, Anne Shelton was to "box her ears as a cursed bastard that she was". Mary also had a habit of eating large breakfasts in her chamber, but Anne Boleyn now ordered that Mary was to be starved back into the Great Hall, where she would eat with other members of the household.[22] Anne Shelton could hardly act upon these instructions, and she treated Mary with "too great kindness and regard", for which she was rebuffed by Anne Boleyn's brother and uncle. With a dose of defiance, Shelton replied that even if Mary "was the bastard daughter of a poor gentleman, her kindness, her

"I am a woman"

modesty, and her virtues called forth all respect and honour".[23] And because Mary was the King's daughter, Anne Shelton was determined to treat her as such.

The changes in her household and separation from her mother worried Mary, who often suffered with what one contemporary termed as "hysteria".[24] The word "hysteria" appeared first in *On the Diseases of Women* in the Hippocratic Corpus. It was considered a disease of the womb, called "hystera" in Greek. The ancient philosopher Plato explained:

"What is called the matrix or womb, a living creature within them (women) with a desire for child-bearing, if it be left long unfruitful beyond the due season, is vexed and aggrieved, and wandering throughout the body and blocking the channels of the breath, by forbidding respiration brings the sufferer to extreme distress and causes all manner of disorders."[25]

Many years later, the Venetian ambassador would report that Mary was prone to bouts of melancholy that were a product of "menstruous retention and suffocation of the matrix [womb]".[26] This disease was believed to be caused by the retention of menstrual fluids. Katharine of Aragon asked the imperial ambassador Chapuys to request of Henry VIII if she could nurse Mary through her sickness because she knew how to treat this kind of an ailment since she suffered from the same complaint, presumably during the time of her penurious widowhood. But the King was adamant and refused. Chapuys asked the King to at least allow Margaret Pole to return to Mary's service for the time of her sickness, but Henry dismissed Margaret as "a fool, of no experience . . . [who] would not have known what to do, whereas her present governess is an expert lady even in such female complaints".[27] As much as she wanted to, Katharine of Aragon was in no position to help her daughter. She herself started suffering with an illness that would eventually lead to her death. Katharine's overall poor physical condition was further exacerbated by recurring visits of the King's councillors, who pressed her to renounce her queenly title and accept that she was Dowager Princess of Wales.

In December 1533, Katharine lost many of her trusted female servants. The imperial ambassador, who still referred to Katharine as Queen, painted a rather gloomy picture of Katharine, stripped of her dignity and placed under a virtual house arrest:

"They [the royal commissioners] had likewise dismissed every female servant, not leaving even one of her chamber maids; but hearing the Queen say and affirm that she would take no others into her service, that she would not undress to go to bed, and would lock the door of her chamber herself, they allowed two of them to remain; not those,

"I am a woman"

however, whom the Queen would gladly have chosen. All the Queen's present servants, with the exception of her confessor, physician, and apothecary, who, as above stated, cannot speak a word of English, have been sworn upon oath not to call her by the title of Queen; against which she duly protested before the Commissioners at the time and afterwards, telling them that she should never repute them as her servants, but merely as guards, since she considered herself a prisoner from that moment."[28]

Yet it is clear that Chapuys was exaggerating. Maria de Salinas, Katharine's Spanish friend "who has remained with her all her life" was allowed to stay with Katharine and serve her at her own expense; she was not dismissed until July 1534.[29] Katharine was prone to exaggeration as well. By April 1535, she was complaining to her nephew Charles V that she was ready to "go sue for alms for the love of God", although she sat at the centre of a household costing Henry VIII a staggering amount of £3,000.[30] The King insisted that she was not his lawful wife but he was a stickler for etiquette and allowed Katharine to retain a respectable train of servants to maintain her royal dignity.

NOTES

[1] *Calendar of State Papers, Venice,* Volume 4, n. 682.
[2] *Calendar of State Papers, Spain,* Volume 4 Part 2, n. 584.

3 Ibid., Volume 4 Part 1, n. 422.

4 Ibid., Volume 4 Part 2, n. 880.

5 Edward Hall, *Hall's Chronicle*, p. 784.

6 Muriel St Clare Byrne, *The Lisle Letters*, Volume 1, p. 332.

7 *Letters and Papers, Foreign and Domestic, Henry VIII*, Volume 6, n. 212.

8 *Calendar of State Papers, Spain*, Volume 4 Part 2, 1531-1533, n. 1057.

9 David Loades, *Elizabeth I: A Life*, p. 26.

10 *Calendar of State Papers, Spain*, Volume 4 Part 1, 1529-1530, n. 354.

11 Susan Walters Schmid, *Anne Boleyn, Lancelot de Carle, and the Uses of Documentary Evidence*, p. 119.

12 G. W. Bernard, *The King's Reformation*, p. 89.

13 John Strype, *Memorials of Archbishop Cranmer*, Volume 1, pp. 332-33.

14 *Letters and Papers, Foreign and Domestic, Henry VIII*, Volume 6, n. 7.

15 Ibid., n. 1468.

16 Ibid., n. 1419.

17 M.A. Everett Wood, *Letters of Royal and Illustrious Ladies of Great Britain*, Volume 2, pp. 98-101.

18 *Letters and Papers, Foreign and Domestic, Henry VIII*, Volume 6, n. 1465.

19 *Letters and Papers, Foreign and Domestic, Henry VIII*, Volume 7, n. 296.

20 *Calendar of State Papers, Spain*, Volume 4 Part 2, n. 1161.

21 Muriel St Clare Byrne, *The Lisle Letters*, Volume 2, p. 45.

22 *Letters and Papers, Foreign and Domestic, Henry VIII*, Volume 7, n. 171.

23 *Calendar of State Papers, Spain*, Volume 5 Part 1, n. 17.

24 *Calendar of State Papers, Venice*, Volume 4, n. 664.

25 James Hillman, *The Myth of Analysis: Three Essays in Archetypal Psychology*, p. 253.

26 *Calendar of State Papers, Venice*, Volume 6, n. 883.

27 *Letters and Papers, Foreign and Domestic, Henry VIII*, Volume 8, n. 263.

28 *Calendar of State Papers, Spain*, Volume 4 Part 2, n. 1165.

29 *Calendar of State Papers, Spain*, Volume 5 Part 1, n. 75.

30 *Letters and Papers, Foreign and Domestic, Henry VIII*, Volume 7, n. 1208.

CHAPTER 5
"OLD TRUSTY WOMEN"

While Katharine of Aragon lingered in the English countryside, Anne Boleyn was trying to carve out her own career as Queen, but she remained deeply unpopular, and even after her coronation people contested her right to wear the crown. In August 1533, a priest from Lancashire disparaged the new Queen in no uncertain terms: "I will have none for queen but Queen Katharine; who the devil made Nan Bullen, that whore, Queen?"[1] He was not the only one who was discontented. The royal commissioners had their hands full interrogating men and women who grudged against Anne Boleyn in the farthest corners of England. One Margaret Chancellor, a spinster from Bradfield St Clare, called the new Queen "a goggle-eyed whore", while a certain Mistress Burgyn told her midwife that "for her honesty and her cunning [skill] she might be midwife unto the Queen of England, if it were Queen Katharine; and if it were Queen Anne, she was too good to be her midwife, for she was a whore and a harlot of her living".[2]

In the early years of their relationship, Henry VIII tried to stifle such public outcries. When the parishioners walked out of a service after an elderly priest recommended praying for "the health and welfare of Queen Anne", the King was "so much disgusted" that he sent an express command to the Lord Mayor of London "that unless he wished to displease him immensely he must take care that the thing did not happen again". The Lord Mayor warned the citizens of London to abstain from murmuring against Henry VIII's marriage to Anne Boleyn and "to command their own journeymen and servants, and still a more difficult task their own wives, to refrain from speaking disparagingly about the new Queen".[3] Women saw Henry VIII's marriage to Anne as an assault on traditional family values and sided with the wronged Katharine of Aragon. People in general were also horrified about the split with Rome and blamed Anne for opening the floodgates of heresy.

Among the courtiers who could not tolerate Anne Boleyn as Queen of England was Gertrude Courtenay, the outspoken Marchioness of Exeter. Her association with the executed Nun of Kent incurred Henry VIII's wrath, but she emerged from this scandal unscathed. Gertrude's loyalty to Katharine of Aragon was her primary agenda, and she soon started her dealings with Eustace Chapuys, Charles V's ambassador. Chapuys's own loyalty to Katharine and her daughter, Mary, was as equally strong as his hatred of Anne Boleyn. The gossipy ambassador befriended all those who supported Katharine and detested Anne, hoping to gain more

"Old trusty women"

information for Charles V. Gertrude was, as Chapuys wrote, "the sole consolation" of Katharine and Mary. She quickly gained his trust and became one of his most valued informants. As the wife of Henry VIII's kinsman—Henry Courtenay was brought up with the King—Gertrude was one of the "great ladies" who served at court during important occasions of state such as coronations and christenings. She thus moved freely between her vast household and lodgings at court, where her husband served as one of the members of the Privy Chamber.[4]

By 1535, the nobility of England were worried that Henry VIII would use drastic measures to bring Katharine of Aragon and her daughter, Mary, to heel. The 1534 Act of Succession was enforced by an oath of allegiance promulgated by parliament in the same year. Refusal was equivalent to treason; the most famous victims of the act were Bishop John Fisher and Sir Thomas More, who were executed in 1535. Mary was pressured to accept the new political and religious situation, but she steadfastly refused to acknowledge Anne Boleyn as Queen. Anne Shelton, Mary's governess, informed Mary that "the King himself has said that he would make her lose her head for violating the laws of his realm".[5] Katharine of Aragon feared that Henry VIII would "immediately put her [Mary] to death, or at least to prison for life", and she often repeated that she believed that she and her daughter might be executed for their defiance.[6] Gertrude Courtenay, whose husband had daily access to the King, sent panicked messages to Chapuys. In November 1535, she appeared in disguise at the doorstep of his private apartments in London, informing him that the King now openly talked about putting Katharine and Mary to death. "These are things too monstrous to be believed", wrote the exasperated Chapuys in one of his dispatches.[7] Chapuys blamed Anne Boleyn for pushing Henry VIII to kill his former wife and daughter, but it would soon become apparent that this was not the case.

In late 1535, Katharine of Aragon's health began to deteriorate, and it became clear to everyone that she was mortally ill. The news about Katharine's illness spread like wildfire across the country, and it soon reached the ears of Maria de Salinas, Lady Willoughby, Katharine's Spanish friend and former lady-in-waiting. "I heard say that my mistress is very sore sick again", she wrote in a letter to Secretary Thomas Cromwell on 30 December 1535. She desired to see Katharine, but she needed a special licence from the King. "I pray you remember me of your goodness", she urged Cromwell, "for you did promise me to labour the King's Grace to get me licence to go to her Grace afore God send for her; for, as I am informed, there is no other likelihood but it shall be shorty".[8] Maria feared that she would be unable to see

"Old trusty women"

Katharine for the last time, but Cromwell was unmoved and failed to reply.

Maria decided to defy both Thomas Cromwell and Henry VIII, and on 1 January 1536, she travelled on horseback through snowy weather to the remote Kimbolton Castle, Katharine of Aragon's residence. She reached her destination at six o'clock in the afternoon and knocked at the castle's doors. Katharine of Aragon's servants were dismayed to see Maria, whom they did not expect. Maria claimed she had a fall from her horse while travelling. She was distressed and, in a bid for sympathy, told Katharine's chamberlain that "she thought never to have seen the Princess Dowager again by reason of such tidings as she had heard of her". But the chamberlain demanded to see the licence, which Maria did not have. "It was ready to be showed", she replied, but when she left Kimbolton that wintry night, after seeing Katharine for the last time, the chamberlain saw neither Maria nor her licence.[9] Katharine of Aragon died six days later, on 7 January 1536, and the King never charged Maria with visiting her royal mistress without his permission.

Katharine of Aragon died surrounded by three of her "old trusty women". We know that there were no Spaniards among them because when Eustace Chapuys visited Katharine on 3 January 1536 and addressed her in Spanish, Sir Edmund

Great Ladies

Bedingfield recorded that these women did not understand the language.[10]

Katharine considered herself the King's wife until the end. The law in England forbade married women to write their last wills, but Katharine dictated a document similar to a testament in which she made several bequests and settled her debts. It is clear that Katharine still owned valuable possessions such as gold and silver jewellery and luxurious gowns she wanted to be made into vestments for a convent of Observant Friars, where she desired to be buried. The bequests in Katharine's last will reveal an intricate network of women who remained loyal to the former Queen, although it is clear that not all of these ladies served Katharine until her death. Katharine's first bequest was to her favourite maid of honour, Elizabeth Darrell, who received £20 "for her marriage".[11] Elizabeth was a daughter of Sir Edward Darrell of Littlecote who served as Katharine of Aragon's vice-chamberlain between 1517 and 1530. He died in March 1530, leaving his daughter under Katharine of Aragon's protection. Elizabeth was one of the eight ladies in Katharine's household who refused to swear an oath to Katharine as Princess Dowager of Wales, arguing that she swore an oath to Katharine as Queen and swearing other oaths would be equal to perjury. After Katharine's death, Elizabeth became the mistress of Sir Thomas Wyatt, the famous Tudor poet, and

"Old trusty women"

found a new employer in the person of Gertrude Courtenay, Marchioness of Exeter. Other women mentioned in Katharine of Aragon's testament were Blanche Twyford, who received £10, Margery Otwell and Dorothy Whiller, who received £10 each, Mary de la Sa, wife of Katharine's Spanish physician, who received £40, and Isabel Vergas, Katharine's Spanish lady-in-waiting, who received £20. There were also "little maidens", "Mistress Isabel, daughter of Mistress Margery" and a laundress.[12]

Little is known about these women except for their names. Some, like Isabel Vergas, who was recorded in the royal household as Katharine's chamberer in 1511, must have been long-term servants, and trusted ones at that. Elizabeth Darrell, Margery Otwell, Blanche Twyford and Dorothy Whiller were among the eight ladies who refused to swear the new oath in 1533; they clearly remained staunchly supportive of Katharine, and it is highly likely that they served her in 1536. Katharine begged the King to safeguard the marriage portions for her unmarried maids, "they being but three", and Henry clearly felt responsible for these women.[13] In November 1539, Blanche Twyford was rewarded with £66 "for her long and painful service done unto the Princess Dowager"; whether other ladies were rewarded in the same manner remains unclear.[14]

NOTES

[1] *Letters and Papers, Foreign and Domestic, Henry VIII*, Volume 6, n. 964.

[2] *Letters and Papers, Foreign and Domestic, Henry VIII*, Volume 7, n. 840. Ibid., Volume 8, n. 196.

[3] *Calendar of State Papers, Spain*, Volume 4 Part 2, n. 1062.

[4] *Letters and Papers, Foreign and Domestic, Henry VIII*, Volume 6, n. 1125.

[5] *Letters and Papers, Foreign and Domestic, Henry VIII*, Volume 7, n. 530.

[6] *Letters and Papers, Foreign and Domestic, Henry VIII*, Volume 8, n. 189.

[7] *Letters and Papers, Foreign and Domestic, Henry VIII*, Volume 9, n. 861.

[8] M.A. Everett Wood, *Letters of Royal and Illustrious Ladies of Great Britain*, Volume 2, pp. 208-9.

[9] *Letters and Papers, Foreign and Domestic, Henry VIII*, Volume 10, n. 28.

[10] Ibid.

[11] Nicholas Harris Nicolas, *Testamenta Vetusta*, Volume 1, p. 37.

[12] Ibid.

[13] Nicholas Harris Nicolas, op. cit.

[14] *Letters and Papers, Foreign and Domestic, Henry VIII*, Volume 14 Part 2, n. 781.

CHAPTER 6
"MESSAGE FROM THE MARCHIONESS"

Within days of Katharine of Aragon's death, Anne Boleyn instructed her aunt, Anne Shelton, the governess of the joint household of the King's daughters, to tell her stepdaughter Mary that if she "would lay aside her obstinacy and obey her father", Anne would become like a "second mother" to her and welcome her to court. Anne assured Mary that she would not return as her servant—"she should be exempted from being her train-bearer, and might walk by her side"—but as a member of the royal family.[1] Anne believed that now, with Katharine of Aragon dead, Mary would finally accept that she was Queen of England. But Anne overestimated Mary, who could not accept Anne as Queen and Elizabeth as princess. She sent panicked letters to Eustace Chapuys, who advised her to change her tactics. Whereas previously Mary said that she could "acknowledge no other Queen but my mother", she was now to say that since the pope decided in 1534 that Henry VIII's marriage to Katharine of Aragon was lawful and his marriage to Anne Boleyn was not, "the Lady Anne could never assume the title of Queen".

Great Ladies

Furthermore, as a good Catholic, Mary was to say that "she could not conscientiously contravene the Pope's commands".[2]

Anne Shelton soon informed Anne that Mary "disregarded entirely the offers made to her in her name and would rather suffer a hundred deaths than change her opinion." Mary's refusal to accept Anne as Queen was the highest insult for Anne, her daughter Elizabeth and everything she stood for. But Anne had the upper hand. She was with child again. In a letter addressed to Anne Shelton and deliberately left at Mary's oratory, Anne informed Lady Shelton that the King planned to bring the matter of his elder daughter's disobedience to an end. Anne explained:

"What I have done has been more for charity than for anything the King or I care what road she takes, or whether she will change her purpose, for if I have a son, as I hope shortly, I know what will happen to her [Mary]; and therefore, considering the Word of God, to do good to one's enemy, I wished to warn her beforehand because I have daily experience that the King's wisdom is such as not to esteem her repentance of her rudeness and unnatural obstinacy when she has no choice."[3]

Anne implied that she gave Mary a chance to accept the political reality because if she had a son, the King would act more decisively and would not tolerate Mary's obstinacy

"Message from the marchioness"

any longer. But Anne's hopes were to be dashed again. On 29 January 1536, on the day of Katharine of Aragon's funeral, she miscarried a son. Henry VIII was shaken to the core and told Anne that he believed that God denied them male heirs. Was it because God was displeased over his second marriage? Anne was, after all, a sister of his former mistress—if it was a sin to marry his brother's widow, wasn't it also a sin to marry a woman with whose sister he had had a sexual relationship?

Caught up in a whirlwind of thoughts about the validity of his second marriage, the King told one of his close friends something that sent shockwaves across the court. Gertrude Courtenay, Marchioness of Exeter, quickly picked up the rumour and sent word to Eustace Chapuys that Henry VIII was considering the repudiation of Anne Boleyn. Gertrude and her husband "were informed by one of the principal persons at court that this King had said to someone in great confidence, and as it were in confession, that he had made this marriage, seduced by sortileges and charms and for this reason he considered it null; and that this was evident because God did not permit them to have any male issue, and that he believed that he might take another wife, which he gave to understand that he had some wish to do".[4] Chapuys could hardly believe this piece of intelligence, but he soon discovered it was true.

Great Ladies

As long as Anne Boleyn enjoyed Henry VIII's favour she was safe, but her inability to produce a male heir, coupled with her domineering personality, drove the King away from her. Anne failed to make the transition from an enchanting mistress into an obedient wife and desired to remain Henry's lover and adviser, but the King hated when she "meddled" with his affairs, both private and political.[5] The moment she lost his favour, she was vulnerable to attacks from her enemies, who started conspiring against her. In April 1536, the imperial ambassador reported that the King was so tired of Anne that "he could not bear her any longer".[6] The Courtenays and the Poles were quick to notice this change of Henry's mood and began plotting. On 1 April 1536, Eustace Chapuys hosted a dinner party at his London residence. Among the eminent guests were Henry Courtenay, Marquess of Exeter, Elizabeth FitzGerald, Dowager Countess of Kildare, and Henry Pole, Lord Montagu. They complained bitterly about "the disorder of affairs" in England and told Chapuys that Anne Boleyn, "the Concubine", was on bad terms with Thomas Cromwell, her erstwhile supporter.[7] They knew very well that Cromwell saw that the King wanted to repudiate Anne and marry a woman he was now in love with.

Henry VIII's new love interest was Jane Seymour, a young lady who served in Anne Boleyn's household. Chapuys saw nothing remarkable about Jane, informing his royal

"Message from the marchioness"

master that she was "not a woman of great wit".[8] She came from a family that enjoyed royal favour—Henry VIII visited her family home at Wolf Hall in 1526 and 1535 while on progress—although the career of the Seymours was undistinguished by great achievements. This all changed the moment Henry VIII set his eyes on Jane, who was "of middle stature and no great beauty, so fair that one would call her rather pale than otherwise".[9] The King was drawn to Jane's mild demeanour and gentle sweetness and began pursuing her. His "love and desire towards the said lady was wonderfully increased" when Jane, with virgin-like modesty, turned down the King's present of a purse filled with money.

Jane soon found out that the anti-Boleyn faction yearned to use her special relationship with the King as a weapon in deposing Anne Boleyn. The most prominent members of the court began to seek her friendship and offered their precious advice. One of them was Gertrude Courtenay, Marchioness of Exeter, who was Eustace Chapuys's informant about Henry's affair with Jane. It was Gertrude who informed the imperial ambassador about the incident with a purse filled with money. It was also Gertrude who told Chapuys that Henry VIII decided to show Jane that he "loved her honourably" and intended to speak with her only with her relatives present.[10] To achieve his purpose, the King placed Jane's elder brother Edward and his wife, Anne, in the lodgings

Great Ladies

belonging to Thomas Cromwell. These lodgings, Gertrude explained, were placed conveniently near a certain gallery that the King could access without being seen by anyone. Jane Seymour was escorted there whenever the King wanted to see her, and she was chaperoned by her brother and sister-in-law.

Anne Boleyn was greatly displeased with her husband's new love affair, and she blamed Jane, whom she had once caught sitting on Henry VIII's knees, for her recent miscarriage. But there was little Anne could do to stop Henry from flirting with Jane, especially since Mistress Seymour was vigorously coached by the Queen's enemies on how to behave with the King. She was advised to cling to her virginity and encouraged "to tell the King boldly how his marriage is detested by the people, and none consider it lawful".[11] This was not an exaggeration. Anne was never popular among the people of England. In October 1535, the French ambassador reported that "the lower people are greatly exasperated against the Queen, saying concerning her a thousand ill and improper things, and also against those who support her in her enterprises".[12] This statement is borne out by many cases of royal commissioners investigating men and women who were caught grudging against Queen Anne in various parts of England.

Whereas the King could stifle the opposition in the countryside, he could hardly do so at court, where political

"Message from the marchioness"

factions competed for his favour. Many nobles, especially those with Plantagenet blood flowing in their veins, were unhappy about the social and religious upheaval generated by Henry VIII's marriage to Anne Boleyn. The Courtenays and the Poles often visited each other and discussed current policies. They believed that the King decided to divorce their "good Queen Katharine" because he was "in the snare of unlawful love with the lady Anne", and mocked the reformed Church of England, seeing it as a by-product of Henry's infatuation with Anne.[13] Anne, who was elevated to the peerage and queenly honour due to Henry VIII's favour, was disparaged as "a harlot and a heretic"; she represented everything the conservative courtiers hated the most.[14]

Anne's leanings towards the evangelical movement were well known. It was Anne who gave Henry her own copy of a banned book entitled *The Obedience of a Christian Man*, wherein William Tyndale argued that popes had no authority over kings. She was interested in distributing the Bible in vernacular and had a copy of Tyndale's English translation of the New Testament on her desk, encouraging her ladies-in-waiting to read it at their leisure. This was a risky move since Henry VIII was hostile to the idea of his subjects reading the Bible in their own language. Henry insisted that the reading of the Bible should be strictly controlled because otherwise people could start to interpret it in their own way.

Great Ladies

The anti-Boleyn faction now clustered around Jane Seymour, who was being groomed to become the next Queen of England. The imperial ambassador observed the unfolding events with a mixture of excitement and exasperation, informing Charles V that Anne Boleyn's cousin, Sir Nicholas Carew, was daily conspiring against her and trying to persuade "Mistress Seymour and other conspirators to accomplish her ruin".[15] Gertrude Courtenay, one of the conspirators, asked Chapuys for his assistance in the plot. Chapuys considered it an honour because he wanted to see Katharine of Aragon's daughter, Mary, reestablished in the line of succession and England purged of "the heretical doctrines and practices" of Anne Boleyn, the detested "concubine". Mary herself was regularly informed about the developments in the case. When Nicholas Carew sent her a messenger to inform her that "her rival would soon be dismissed", Mary was glad, even if her father's remarriage meant that she would be supplanted in the succession by any prospective sons Jane Seymour might bear.[16] Chapuys conferred with Mary, who instructed him to "watch the proceedings, and if possible help to accomplish the said divorce". On her part, Mary was eager to emphasize that she did not wish for the King's divorce from Anne Boleyn "out of revenge for the many injuries inflicted on her mother, the late Queen, and on herself" because she had forgotten and forgiven them "for the honour of God, and she now bore no ill-will to anyone whomsoever".[17]

"Message from the marchioness"

The conspirators often used the words "dismiss" and "divorce" interchangeably when speaking about Anne's ruin. This clearly points out that they expected Henry VIII to divorce Anne Boleyn and send her away from court. Just when the conspiracy turned deadly remains unknown, but Thomas Cromwell soon began interrogating Anne's ladies-in-waiting, hoping to build a case against the Queen.

NOTES

[1] *Calendar of State Papers, Spain,* Volume 5 Part 2, n. 9.

[2] Ibid.

[3] *Letters and Papers, Foreign and Domestic, Henry VIII,* Volume 10, n. 307.

[4] *Letters and Papers, Foreign and Domestic, Henry VIII,* Volume 10, n. 199.

[5] In 1536, Henry warned Jane Seymour "not to meddle with his affairs" or else she would end up like "the late Queen [Anne Boleyn]". *Letters and Papers, Foreign and Domestic, Henry VIII,* Volume 11, July-December 1536, n. 860.

[6] *Calendar of State Papers, Spain,* Volume 5 Part 2, n. 47.

[7] *Letters and Papers, Foreign and Domestic, Henry VIII,* Volume 10, n. 601.

[8] Ibid., n. 901.

[9] Ibid.

[10] *Letters and Papers, Foreign and Domestic, Henry VIII,* Volume 10, n. 601.

[11] Ibid.

[12] *Letters and Papers, Foreign and Domestic, Henry VIII,* Volume 9, n. 566.

[13] *Letters and Papers, Foreign and Domestic, Henry VIII,* Volume 13 Part 2, n. 800.

[14] Ibid.

[15] *Calendar of State Papers, Spain,* Volume 5 Part 2, n. 47.

[16] Ibid.

[17] Ibid., n. 48.

CHAPTER 7
"THE FIRST ACCUSERS"

The loss of her unborn son in 1536 was not only a personal tragedy for Anne Boleyn and Henry VIII, but "a great discomfort to this entire realm", as one chronicler perceptively noted.[1] The Queen was recuperating within her private apartments with a handful of her favourite female servants at Greenwich Palace while the King moved to Whitehall. The imperial ambassador Chapuys attributed this separation to Henry VIII's displeasure with Anne, but the Queen's bill for apothecary services, which amounted to a staggering £41, makes it clear that she needed to recover her health after a dangerous miscarriage. The loss of a son was painful, but it did not spell out the end of Anne's childbearing years. Chapuys soon picked up a rumour that Anne was comforting her ladies-in-waiting, telling them that she hoped to be with child again soon. These women were privy to Anne's secrets, and she treated them as members of her family. One of her favourite ladies was Elizabeth Somerset, Countess of Worcester. The countess served Anne well before she became Queen, and the two shared a relationship close enough for Anne to pay for the countess's midwife and lend her the large sum of £100. Elizabeth Somerset, who was herself pregnant when Anne lost

"The first accusers"

her baby, empathised with the Queen so much so that Anne believed that the countess's "child did not stir in her body" because of "the sorrow she took for me".[2] Yet it was Elizabeth Somerset who, in May 1536, was one of the three ladies-in-waiting who accused the Queen of immorality.

Anne Boleyn's court was vibrant and her ladies mostly young. When Sir William Kingston visited the court while Anne still presided over it by the King's side, he noted that "here is much youth and I am but in the midst of mine age".[3] In her mid-thirties, the Queen struck a glamorous figure among her young courtiers, but the insecurity of her position as well as the unexpected loss of her son rendered her older than she truly was. Although the imperial ambassador described her as thin and old, it is clear that Anne's circle found her appearance attractive and company stimulating. She loved music and poetry and excelled in singing and dancing. Men often wrote poetry for her and competed for her favour. When Sir Thomas More's daughter briefly visited the court, she was appalled to learn that there was nothing else "but dancing and sporting".[4] Anne's enemies delighted in passing the stories about dancing parties she held in her private chambers, her frequent fashion innovations and "such corporal delights in which she had a special grace".[5]

Yet it is clear that Anne's life was not all fun and games. She was known to have been a pious Catholic with evangelical leanings. Some, like the imperial ambassador, wrote that Anne and her family were "more Lutheran than Luther himself", but it is evident that Anne was not a Protestant, as this term was not coined until after her death.[6] It is clear that Anne opted for reforming the abuses and superstitions within the Church and allowing her subjects to read the Bible in vernacular. She was also devoted to charity. Anne employed her ladies-in-waiting to sew and distribute shirts for the poor and carried a purse filled with money with her in case she met the needy while travelling. Not everyone believed that Anne's motives were pure though. The imperial ambassador had heard a rumour that Anne attributed Katharine of Aragon's enormous popularity with the ordinary people to large alms she was accustomed to distribute, and she decided to surpass her rival.

Most ladies-in-waiting who served Anne Boleyn in her Privy Chamber were her trusted friends. Elizabeth Somerset, Anne Cobham, Margery Horsman, Mary Shelton, Mary Howard, Mary Zouche, Elizabeth Holland, Mary Carey and Jane Boleyn formed the core of the Queen's household. In 1534, Mary Carey, Anne's widowed sister, was dismissed from her post when she married beneath her station without obtaining a royal licence. She wrote a pitiful letter to Thomas Cromwell wherein she urged him to intercede on her behalf with her family and especially with Anne, but it remains unknown whether she was allowed to return to court before her royal

"The first accusers"

sister's death. Also Anne's sister-in-law, Jane Boleyn, was banished in 1534 after the King discovered her involvement in an intrigue aimed at dismissing his mistress from court. But whereas some members of her family let her down, others thrived in her household. Anne's young cousin Mary Howard, Duchess of Richmond, was "the chief and principal of her waiting maids" and retained fond memories of the Queen.[7] Towards the end of her life, Anne developed a "great friendship" with Margery Horsman, who was responsible for the delivery of Anne's gowns from the Great Wardrobe.[8]

During the spring of 1536, the strength of Anne Boleyn's friendship with her ladies-in-waiting was to be tested because, at that time, Thomas Cromwell began a series of secret interrogations of the Queen's servants. Anne may have noticed that her ladies disappeared for hours on end only to reemerge with serious and shaken expressions on their faces, unwilling to talk. They were examined "in most secret sort" so as not to raise the Queen's suspicions, yet Anne was aware that something sinister was happening around her.[9] Some six days before her arrest, she took her favourite chaplain aside and entrusted her daughter's spiritual well-being to his care. Matthew Parker never forgot Anne's troubled expression and the hushed tone of her voice and promised to keep an eye on Elizabeth.

Great Ladies

On 2 May 1536, Anne Boleyn was arrested and taken by barge from Greenwich Palace to the Tower of London. She was accused of committing incest with her brother, taking numerous lovers and inciting them to assassinate Henry VIII. Cromwell later claimed that Anne's immoral living was so apparent that the "ladies of her Privy Chamber and her chamberers could not contain it within their breasts".[10] Just what the ladies confessed remains unclear. John Husee, a seasoned courtier, tried to discover what really happened, but everything was so "discreetly spoken" that he could hardly learn anything of substance. Some ladies were said to have been the chief among the Queen's accusers: "the Lady Worcester, and Nan Cobham, with one maid more".[11] Only Elizabeth Somerset, Countess of Worcester, can be identified without doubt. The Nan Cobham mentioned in the letter may have been Anne Brooke, Baroness Cobham, who received a summons to attend Anne Boleyn's coronation in 1533. Historian Eric Ives suggested that the "one maid more" may have been Margery Horsman, but it seems unlikely since during the interrogation she acted "strangely" and refused to heap slanders onto her royal mistress.[12] Just what these ladies told Cromwell remains unclear. According to a poem written by Lancelot de Carle, who served as the French ambassador's secretary, the Countess of Worcester told her brother that Anne Boleyn was entertaining men in her chambers late into the night and had carnal relations with her brother and with

"The first accusers"

Mark Smeaton, the talented courtly musician. Strangely enough, none of these women testified against the Queen in an open court, as was customary when the accused denied their guilt.

Among many indiscretions laid at Anne Boleyn's feet, several seem to have occurred within her Privy Chamber. Anne and George were said to have mocked the King's poetry and clothes, and George in particular was accused of making bawdy jokes touching on his niece's paternity. Anne also told her sister-in-law that Henry VIII had "neither the skill nor virility" as a lover, and it was reported that she could "never love the King in her heart" and appeared tired of married life with him.[13] Henry VIII was especially annoyed at these charges which, to him, amounted to a "great crime" because they questioned his manhood and talents.[14] During the trial, Anne Boleyn was accused of "following daily her frail and carnal lust" and enticing the King's servants to "violate her". Henry Norris, Francis Weston, William Brereton and Mark Smeaton were said to have been her lovers, and even her brother was accused of knowing her carnally on many occasions, "sometimes by his own procurement and sometimes by the Queen's".[15] None of Anne Boleyn's ladies-in-waiting were accused of facilitating these clandestine meetings, and it was implied that the Queen planned them herself.

Great Ladies

Judge John Spelman, who presided over the trials, mentioned only one lady-in-waiting, Bridget Wingfield, whose deathbed testimony, now lost, was presented as evidence of Anne Boleyn's misdemeanour. Bridget was conveniently dead and could hardly have been privy to all of the meetings between Anne and her putative lovers mentioned in the indictment. Thomas Cromwell himself later admitted that some evidence was destroyed and never presented at court. The reason, Cromwell claimed, was the shocking nature of the confessions, but it is more likely that there were no confessions at all. Only Mark Smeaton confessed to have known the Queen carnally, but he might have been tortured or promised pardon. The others maintained their innocence until the end.

Anne and her brother were tried separately, but both remained calm and defended themselves admirably. Despite their efforts, both were condemned to die as traitors and adulterers. Shortly before her death, Anne took the holy sacrament and affirmed on the damnation of her soul that she had never committed misconduct. This was her last attempt, after pleading not guilty at her trial, to clear her name from slander.

On 17 May 1536, Anne's putative lovers were executed with an axe on the Tower Hill, and the Queen followed them to death two days later. On the morning of 19 May 1536, the

"The first accusers"

Queen made a short walk from her luxurious apartments in the Tower to the high wooden scaffold prepared for her execution. Among the ladies who accompanied her were four young damsels who appeared distressed. Shortly after her arrest, four ladies whom she "never loved" had been appointed as Anne's servants.[16] Because the female servants who escorted Anne to the scaffold were described as "young", and the women who lodged with her in the Tower were middle-aged by Tudor standards, there is a possibility that the King allowed Anne to pick her favourite ladies to be with her in her last hour.[17]

When she mounted the scaffold, Anne Boleyn faced a crowd of one thousand spectators who had come to see her head roll. She remained composed, but her voice broke several times during her final speech. She refrained from accusing anyone and praised the King as a good and merciful lord. "And if any person will meddle of my cause", she urged, "I require them to judge the best". She asked the gathered people to pray for her and then kneeled. Her ladies removed her ermine mantle, took away her jewellery, tucked her dark locks under her linen cap and blindfolded her. She prayed fervently before the skilled executioner from Calais cut off her head with one stroke of a sharp sword. The four ladies who watched their Queen's lifeless body collapsing to the ground were "nearly dead themselves from languor and extreme weakness".[18]

Great Ladies

Anne Boleyn was the first Queen of England to be executed. No one could have imagined at that unbearable moment that she would not be the last.

NOTES

[1] *Wriothesley's Chronicle*, Volume 2, p. 70.

[2] *Letters and Papers, Foreign and Domestic, Henry VIII*, Volume 10, n. 793.

[3] Muriel St Clare Byrne, *The Lisle Letters*, Volume 4, p. 196.

[4] Cresacre More, *The Life of Sir Thomas More*, p. 244.

[5] Henry Clifford, *The Life of Jane Dormer, Duchess of Feria*, p. 78.

[6] *Letters and Papers, Foreign and Domestic, Henry VIII*, Volume 5, n. 148.

[7] Rev. M. Hobart Seymour (ed.), *The Actes and Monuments by John Foxe*, p. 372.

[8] *Letters and Papers, Foreign and Domestic, Henry VIII*, Volume Volume 10, n. 799.

[9] Roger B. Merriman, *Life and Letters of Thomas Cromwell*, Volume 1, pp. 11-12.

[10] Ibid.

[11] Muriel St Clare Byrne, *The Lisle Letters*, Volume 3, p. 378.

[12] *Letters and Papers, Foreign and Domestic, Henry VIII*, Volume Volume 10, n. 799.

[13] Ibid., n. 876.

[14] Ibid., n. 908.

[15] Ibid., n. 876.

[16] Ibid., n. 797.

[17] Ibid., n. 911.

[18] Susan Walters Schmid, *Anne Boleyn, Lancelot de Carle, and the Uses of Documentary Evidence*, p. 174.

CHAPTER 8
"MANY ANCIENT LADIES AND GENTLEWOMEN"

Henry VIII married Jane Seymour on 30 May 1536 in the Queen's closet at Whitehall Palace. The King's marriage to Jane was welcomed by conservatives who helped place her on the throne and now expected her to fulfil their high expectations. Jane was to act as a peacemaker and reconcile Henry VIII with his elder daughter, Mary, who now anxiously awaited an invitation to her father's court. Jane talked to the King about the possibility of reinstating Mary to the succession before they married, but Henry VIII retorted that she was a fool and warned her that she should think about the exaltation of her own future children. The King's attitude towards his daughter's disobedient behaviour did not change after the wedding, and he pressured Mary to sign the oath acknowledging that her parents' marriage was void and she was a bastard. The threat of imprisonment loomed large over Mary, who was advised even by her staunch champion, Eustace Chapuys, to relent and sign. Jane Seymour, in whom the conservatives placed their hopes, could not convince the King that Mary should be spared this humiliation and was "rudely repulsed" by Henry.[1] It was a rude awakening for

Great Ladies

Mary, who believed for years that her father was manipulated by Anne Boleyn and would welcome her with open arms after her stepmother's execution. "I perceived that nobody durst speak for me as long as that woman lived", she wrote to Thomas Cromwell shortly after Anne's death.[2] Mary was allowed to return to court only after she humbled herself before her royal father and signed the oath renouncing her rights and admitting that her parents' marriage was illegal. The new Act of Succession was passed in July 1536, declaring both of Henry VIII's daughters illegitimate and allowing the King to designate his own successor.

Jane Seymour was only some eight years older than her new stepdaughter, but she surrounded herself with a throng of "many ancient ladies and gentlewomen" to emphasize that her court was different than her predecessor's.[3] She welcomed those elderly gentlewomen who lingered in obscurity during Anne Boleyn's tenure as Queen and allowed them a great deal of influence. By the end of June 1536, Margaret Pole, Countess of Salisbury, was back at court and shown great favour, although the fact that a large crowd of five thousand people lined the streets to welcome her annoyed the King. The Countess was so influential with the new Queen that Lady Honor Lisle, who actively campaigned to place her daughters in Jane Seymour's household, was encouraged to cultivate her good graces with gifts and letters. Margaret

"Many ancient ladies and gentlewomen"

returned to court because the King expected that her son, Reginald Pole, would send his long-anticipated opinion concerning Henry VIII's divorce and break with Rome. Pole was educated at the King's expense and owed much to him, but he left England for Italy in the early 1530s when he realized he would soon have to take a stance in the King's divorce case. Staunchly Catholic and disappointed with the course of Henry VIII's actions, Reginald Pole penned a treatise entitled *Defence of the Unity of the Church*, wherein he addressed the King directly. Pole's *Defence* defined his views on papal authority and the King's succession and praised those who died for their refusal to accept Henry's supremacy over the Church of England. It was highly personal in nature, and the King perceived it as an attack, not only on his religious and domestic policies but on his royal person. Henry had immediately conceived such hatred towards Reginald Pole that he decided to hunt him down and make him "eat his own heart".[4]

Margaret Pole, whose relationship with the King was already fraught with difficulties due to her staunch support for his daughter Mary, became a casualty of Henry VIII's wrath. When Reginald's *Defence* reached England in the summer of 1536, the King summoned Margaret for an audience and relayed the content of her son's vitriolic treatise in person. Margaret was shocked and immediately wrote to Reginald

Great Ladies

berating him for his attack on the King. "Do your duty or you will be my undoing", she ended prophetically.[5]

Jane Seymour's household was appointed by early June 1536. It was a swift transition because the new Queen retained Anne Boleyn's household officers and ladies-in-waiting, who were required to swear an oath to Jane as their royal mistress. One of the ladies who remained highly in favour was Margery Horsman. On 27 January 1537, she married Michael Lister, and they were jointly appointed as Keepers of the Queen's Jewels.[6] Another lady who managed to ingratiate herself with the Queen was Jane Boleyn, Viscountess Rochford, widow of George Boleyn. The execution of her husband in May 1536 left her destitute, and she wrote a letter to Thomas Cromwell asking him to intercede on her behalf with the King. Cromwell's reaction was swift, and, together with Henry VIII, he ordered Thomas Boleyn to augment his daughter-in-law's living. Lady Rochford received £100 of annual income and a post within Jane Seymour's household. She was held in some esteem by the Queen as evidenced by the presence of Jane's name in the catalogue of Jane Seymour's jewels distributed to her ladies-in-waiting.

One of the most influential ladies in Jane Seymour's household was the Queen's sister-in-law, Anne. Anne Seymour, née Stanhope, had married Jane's brother Edward at some point in 1535. She served as Katharine of Aragon's maid

"Many ancient ladies and gentlewomen"

of honour and was perhaps retained by Anne Boleyn, although the direct evidence is lacking; she may have been the "Mrs Stanhope" recorded in the New Year gift roll for 1534.[7] In March 1536, Edward Seymour was appointed as one of the members of Henry VIII's Privy Chamber and received comfortable lodgings at court. His sister's marriage to the King elevated him socially, and he was created Viscount Beauchamp on 5 June 1536. Anne Seymour, Lady Beauchamp, was believed to have been very influential with the Queen, who showered her with jewels and stood as godmother to Anne's first child in February 1537.

It was a widely held belief that Henry VIII's marriage to Jane Seymour would herald the King's return to the Catholic Church, but it was not to be so. Much to his subjects' disappointment, the King continued his religious policies. In the autumn of 1536, an insurrection known as the Pilgrimage of Grace broke out in the northern parts of England. The rebellion strongly opposed the Dissolution of the Monasteries and the policies of the King's chief minister, Thomas Cromwell. Born and raised a Catholic, Jane Seymour sympathised with the rebels, as evidenced by a dramatic gesture she dared to make in October 1536. The French ambassador, Charles de Marillac, reported that "at the beginning of the insurrection the Queen threw herself on her knees before the King and begged him to restore the abbeys" but was rudely put down.

Great Ladies

Henry VIII warned her not to "meddle with his affairs", invoking the fate of Anne Boleyn. This was "enough to frighten a woman who is not very secure", observed Marillac.[8]

Rumours of the impending coronation of Jane Seymour spread through court shortly after the wedding, but it soon became apparent that the King did not plan to crown his wife before she proved herself fertile. Weeks were turning into months, and the Queen was still not pregnant, her position becoming precarious. In July 1536, just as the new Act of Succession passed through parliament, allowing the King to designate his own successor, Henry VIII's much beloved bastard son Henry FitzRoy died at the age of seventeen. Many believed that the King wanted FitzRoy to become his heir, but the boy's death destroyed these plans. By autumn of 1536, the King was depressed and started wondering if his wife would be able to give him a son. Henry began to make much of his daughter Mary, who was now "the first after the Queen".[9] The King was heard saying that "since his Queen would not give him a son", he wanted to marry his elder daughter to Dom Louis of Portugal so that Mary could give birth to a male heir who would become Henry VIII's successor.[10] Jane Seymour must have been horrified to hear that the King doubted her fertility so openly, knowing how the lack of a male heir contributed to her predecessor's downfall. Yet Henry VIII's fears were unnecessary since his wife conceived during the

"Many ancient ladies and gentlewomen"

winter of 1537. By Corpus Christi Day, her condition was widely celebrated at court when she signified her status as a pregnant woman by loosening up her gown and adjusting her expanding girth by using pins at her stomacher, a decorative panel placed on a whalebone corset.

Unlike her predecessors, who much favoured Greenwich Palace and chose it for their confinements, Jane Seymour decided to establish her birthing chamber at the newly refurbished Hampton Court. She withdrew from public life in anticipation of her child's birth on 16 September 1537 and delivered a long-awaited son at two o'clock in the morning on 12 October. Her labour dragged on for two long days and three nights until the boy was safely delivered. Nicholas Sander, writing in 1585, claimed that "the travail of the Queen being very difficult, the King was asked which of the two lives was to be spared; he answered, the boy's, because he could easily provide himself with other wives."[11] According to this hostile account, Henry VIII was willing to sacrifice the life of Jane Seymour to save his child, but there is nothing in contemporary records to support Sander's assertion. Although Jane Seymour's delivery was long and painful, she was strong enough to sign the letters announcing her son's birth. It was a triumphant occasion for the Queen, who succeeded where Anne Boleyn had failed. Her son was named Edward because

Great Ladies

he was born on the eve of the feast of the translation of Edward the Confessor.

The royal couple chose the godmother of their son before Edward's birth. Their choice fell on the fifty-year-old Margaret Grey, Dowager Marchioness of Dorset. She was the mother of Henry Grey, third Marquess of Dorset, who married Henry VIII's niece Frances Brandon in 1533. Margaret herself was deemed a member of the royal family since she was married to Thomas Grey, second Marquess of Dorset, a grandson of Elizabeth Woodville. The marchioness lived away from court and received a summons to come to Hampton Court Palace on the day of Prince Edward's birth. She was overjoyed and penned a grateful letter to the King:

"It may please your Highness to be advertised, that I have received the Queen's Grace's letters, of the most joyful news and glad tidings that come to England these many years; for the which we all, your Grace's poor subjects, are most bounden to give thanks to Almighty God, that it hath pleased Him of his great mercy so to remember your Grace with a prince, and us all, your poor subjects, to the great comfort, universal weal and quietness of this your whole realm; beseeching Almighty God to send His Grace good life and long, to his pleasure and comfort of your most noble Grace . . ."[12]

"Many ancient ladies and gentlewomen"

The marchioness expressed her gratitude for such a prestigious post, but she was not allowed to come anywhere near the newly born prince. Just as she was moving towards Hampton Court, the plague was raging in London, harvesting three to four lives daily. Margaret stayed at the Archbishop of Canterbury's residence at Croydon, where two persons fell sick, although the cause of their sickness was not yet ascertained. The King, who was mortally afraid of any form of sickness, forbade Margaret to come to court and appointed his daughter Mary as the prince's godmother. Margaret naturally understood that she could not possibly endanger the life of the infant prince and took the news graciously, although she wrote that "it much grieved me that my fortune is so evil, by reason of the sickness here in Croydon".[13]

The christening was a lavish ceremony held in the royal chapel at Hampton Court. A large octagonal platform was raised in the centre of the chapel so that everyone could see the King of England's heir being anointed by the Archbishop of Canterbury. After the ceremony was over, Edward was carried to his parents, who traditionally did not take part in the christening, but awaited him in the antechamber, where the prince received the "blessing of Almighty God, our Lady, and St George, and his father and mother".[14]

Great Ladies

Jane Seymour was sat upright in bed, propped against richly embroidered cushions and tightly wrapped in ermine fur for warmth, wearing a gown of purple velvet. She seemed strong and healthy enough to be participating in the post-baptismal ceremony, and plans were made for her imminent churching. But that same evening, the Queen began feeling unwell and took to her bed. Day by day, she grew increasingly weak until, on 24 October 1537, she had "a natural lax", loosening of the bowels, after which it looked like she was on the road to full recovery.[15] But Jane's condition worsened that night, and in the morning her confessor came to administer the extreme unction. She was dead before midnight.

Jane Seymour's death was a heavy blow to Henry VIII, who had planned a series of jousts and tournaments to celebrate the birth of his son. He was robbed of delight when "Divine Providence has mingled my joy with the bitterness of the death of her who brought me to this happiness".[16]

Jane's death removed her calming, gentle effect on the King, who started descending into paranoid fears for the continuity of his succession. Such fears were justified to some extent because, shortly after Edward's birth, wild rumours spread across the country that Henry VIII and the prince were both dead. By now, the years of misuse of his body and the dangerous fall he suffered when jousting on 24 January 1536 were beginning to show on his ever-expanding frame. The

"Many ancient ladies and gentlewomen"

King's legs had a tendency to swell, and they were covered in fistulas. In 1538, one of the fistulas closed up, and the King remained speechless for almost two weeks, "black in the face and in great danger". The royal physicians lanced the fistula with a red-hot poker, allowing drainage of the "humours" and saving the King's life. From that point on, the fistulas were kept open for the King's safety, producing a putrid stench that could be identified three rooms away, often announcing Henry's arrival.[17] As his health deteriorated, the King started to regard his Pole and Courtenay relatives with suspicion. He once told the French ambassador that he wanted to exterminate the White Rose party, as he referred to his maternal relatives. Rumours swirled abroad that Reginald Pole desired to marry Lady Mary because they were both of noble blood and Catholic.[18] This was the kind of talk Henry VIII feared, and he started regarding his relatives as potential rivals to his throne.

In August 1538, Reginald Pole's younger brother Geoffrey was arrested and placed in the Tower of London, where he was kept in a dank cell. Under severe interrogations, he implicated his brother Henry Pole, Baron Montague, Henry Courtenay and his wife Gertrude, Marquess and Marchioness of Exeter, and Edward Neville. Everything these families talked about in private was now dragged out into the open. Their choice utterances were highly unfavourable to the King

113

and constituted treason under the 1534 Treasons Act. "The King is not dead, but he will one day die suddenly; his leg will kill him and then we shall have jolly stirring", Baron Montague once boasted, mocking the King's chronically ill health and predicting his death. "I never loved him from childhood", he said on another occasion while adding ominously that "he [the King] will be out of his wit one day".[19] The men were accused of secret communication with Reginald Pole and planning to employ the emperor's help in invading England. "Brother, I like well the proceedings of my brother Reginald Pole", Geoffrey Pole once said, adding that he did not like "the doings and proceedings in this realm, and I trust to see a change of this world". If misconstrued, the "change of this world" could imply the change of political regime.[20]

By 4 November 1538, Henry Courtenay, his wife Gertrude and their twelve-year-old son Edward had been arrested and placed in the Tower. Exeter was deemed guilty by association with the Pole brothers. He was accused of saying that "knaves rule about the King. I trust to give them a buffet one day", although what the said "buffet" meant remains unclear.[21] The elderly Margaret Pole was interrogated within her own house and searched, and later taken to the Tower also. Margaret, as the mother of Reginald, Henry and Geoffrey, was accused of abetting their treason while Gertrude and her husband were accused of hearing reports from the

"Many ancient ladies and gentlewomen"

Continent and receiving news about Reginald Pole's doings through their servants.

The King turned his rage against Gertrude, whom he accused of turning his daughter Mary against him, and reminded her that she had narrowly escaped penalty in 1534 when she contacted the Nun of Kent.[22] But Gertrude was the only one, next to Geoffrey Pole, who tried to commit suicide twice after he realized his relatives and friends were to be executed, who escaped with her life. She was pardoned on 21 December 1539 and granted £100 of annuity.

Other members of the White Rose party were not so lucky. Gertrude's husband, Henry Courtenay, and Margaret Pole's son Henry, Baron Montague, were executed on 9 December 1538. It is clear that the King was desperate to get rid of them to punish Reginald Pole. "Pity it is that the folly of one brainsick Pole, or, to say better, of one witless fool, should be the ruin of so great a family", mused Thomas Cromwell before the arrests took place.[23] "I heard you say once after you had seen that furious invective of Cardinal Pole [*Defence*]", wrote Henry VIII's chaplain after the executions, "that you would make him to eat his own heart, which you have now".[24] These remarks make it clear that Henry VIII was driven by personal vengeance. Even the "little nephew of Cardinal Pole" was to suffer the consequences of being related to Reginald. Whereas Edward Courtenay, Gertrude's only son, was allowed

Great Ladies

freedom of movement within the Tower and received a tutor, Henry Pole, Baron Montague's heir, was "poorly and strictly kept and not desired to know anything".[25] He disappeared from the records shortly after 1542.

As to the elderly Margaret Pole, Countess of Salisbury, she was left in the Tower of London, not knowing what would happen to her. She lacked proper apparel and soon complained that she had no warm clothes. She would stay in the Tower until her own execution on 27 May 1541. There was no trial, not even a warning before the execution. Aged sixty-seven at the time of her death, she was the last Plantagenet at the Tudor court. A young, inexperienced executioner was said to have "hacked her head and shoulders to pieces".[26]

NOTES

[1] *Letters and Papers, Foreign and Domestic, Henry VIII,* Volume 11, n. 7.
[2] Ibid., Volume 10, n. 968.
[3] Muriel St Clare Byrne, *The Lisle Letters,* Volume 4, p. 196.
[4] *Letters and Papers, Foreign and Domestic, Henry VIII,* Volume 13 Part 2, n. 1036.
[5] *The Correspondence of Reginald Pole,* p. 119.
[6] *Letters and Papers, Foreign and Domestic, Henry VIII,* Volume 12 Part 2, n. 1150.
[7] TNA E 101/421/13
[8] *Letters and Papers, Foreign and Domestic, Henry VIII,* Volume 11, n. 860.
[9] Ibid.
[10] *Calendar of State Papers, Spain,* Volume 5 Part 2, n. 116.
[11] Nicholas Sander, *The Rise and Growth of the Anglican Schism,* p. 138.
[12] M.A. Everett Wood, *Letters of Royal and Illustrious Ladies of Great Britain,* Volume 2, pp. 342-3.

"Many ancient ladies and gentlewomen"

[13] Ibid.

[14] *Literary Remains of King Edward the Sixth*, p. cclvi.

[15] Peter Heylyn, *Ecclesia restaurata*, Volume 1, p. 15.

[16] *Letters and Papers, Foreign and Domestic, Henry VIII*, Volume 12 Part 2, June-December 1537, n. 972.

[17] Chalmers, C.R. and E.J. Chaloner, "500 Years Later: Henry VIII, Leg Ulcers and the Course of History", *Journal of the Royal Society of Medicine*, 102 (2009), pp. 513-17.

[18] He was not ordained priest until he was raised to the cardinalate in 1539.

[19] *Letters and Papers, Foreign and Domestic, Henry VIII*, Volume 13 Part 2, n. 979.

[20] Ibid.

[21] Ibid.

[22] He was apparently unaware of her secret dealings with the imperial ambassador Eustace Chapuys.

[23] *Letters and Papers, Foreign and Domestic, Henry VIII*, Volume 12 Part 2, n. 795.

[24] *Letters and Papers, Foreign and Domestic, Henry VIII*, Volume 13 Part 2, n. 1036.

[25] *Letters and Papers, Foreign and Domestic, Henry VIII*, Volume 16, n. 1011.

[26] Ibid., n. 897.

CHAPTER 9
"CONTINUANCE IN THE KING'S FAVOUR"

In January 1539, the terrified French ambassador Castillon begged to be recalled from the English court. He feared that Henry VIII, "the most dangerous and cruel man in the world", would try to hurt him if he discovered that the French King had no intention of allying with him. "He is in a fury", Castillon wrote in some perplexity, "and has neither reason nor understanding left".[1] By the time Castillon sat down to compose this dispatch, Henry VIII was gaining a notorious reputation as a monarch. He unleashed a reign of terror onto his subjects, who tiptoed around him, fearing to offend him in any way. But one thing that was constant about Henry VIII was his unabated desire to bask in the attention of beautiful women. Two years had passed since Jane Seymour's death, and the King was still single, but he was always surrounded by a bevy of beautiful young ladies who competed for his favour. One such lady was Anne Basset, a stepdaughter of Arthur Plantagenet, Viscount Lisle and comptroller of Calais.

"Continuance in the King's favour"

The exceptionally good-looking Anne Basset joined the royal household on 16 September 1537, the day Jane Seymour entered her confinement chambers, never to emerge from them again. The Queen had certain reservations about employing Anne as her maid of honour because the girl was not yet sixteen, the minimum age required to receive the post, and she was too French in her manners and appearance for Jane's taste. Anne's mother, Lady Honor Lisle, sent her to be educated in the household of her upper-class French friends, knowing that being French was in vogue when Anne Boleyn was Henry VIII's wife. Lady Lisle doubtlessly groomed her beautiful daughter to become as elegant and as French as Anne Boleyn, but the Queen's unexpected execution put a stop to such plans. Anne Basset's Frenchness suddenly became an obstacle to a court career. Jane Seymour banned the seductive French fashions and returned to the typically English apparel. Jane doubtless feared that the young and beautiful Anne would appeal to her royal husband's taste and delayed her final decision, but eventually she agreed to employ Anne Basset as her maid of honour.

After Jane Seymour's death, her ladies-in-waiting had to seek employment elsewhere. Anne Basset joined the household of her relative, Mary Radcliffe, Countess of Sussex, but she was very much on the King's mind. Although there was no prospect of Henry VIII remarrying immediately after Jane

Great Ladies

Seymour's death, he made Anne a promise that she would retain her hard-won position as maid of honour in the household of his next wife "whenever the time comes".[2] The King clearly missed the presence of women at court because he invited a selected group of ladies to pay a visit to Portsmouth in August 1539. The ladies went to see the King's ships, including the "Great Ship", presumably *Henry Grace a Dieu*. In a letter addressed to Henry VIII, they made cordial thanks for the opportunity. The ships were "so goodly to behold that in our lives we have not seen (excepting your royal person and my lord the Prince your son) a more pleasant sight".[3] Among the signatories were ladies whose husbands served the King faithfully for years: Mabel FitzWilliam, Countess of Southampton, wife of William FitzWilliam, Lord Privy Seal; Alice Browne, wife of Sir Anthony Browne, the King's Master of the Horse; Margaret Howard, wife of Lord William Howard, ambassador to Scotland and France; Joan Denny, wife of Anthony Denny, the King's Groom of the Stool; Jane Mewtas, wife of Peter Mewtas, member of the Privy Chamber, and Elizabeth Tyrwhitt, wife of Robert Tyrwhitt, Esquire of the Body. Other ladies included Margaret Tailboys, daughter-in-law of the King's erstwhile mistress Bessie Blount; Anne Knyvett, Elizabeth Harvey and, of course, Anne Basset.

"Continuance in the King's favour"

The young Anne was held in special esteem by the King, as evidenced by a letter she sent to her mother shortly after the exciting visit to Portsmouth. The King gave her a fine horse and riding saddle, presumably so she could join him on hunting expeditions.[4] Anne clearly had the King's ear because her mother ordered her to obtain pardon for her friend and client John Harris. When she fell sick, the King commanded her to remove from court to Joan Denny's house so she could enjoy "fair walks and a good open air" in the garden.[5] The level of Henry's personal interest in Anne indicates that she may have been his mistress at the time.

Anne Basset soon found out that she would be able to renew her position in the royal household as maid of honour to Henry VIII's fourth wife. After scouring Europe in search of a perfect bride, Henry VIII decided to marry Anne, the sister of William, Duke of Cleves. The King fell madly in love with a portrait of Anne of Cleves executed by his court painter, Hans Holbein, and was excited to bring her to England as soon as possible. Anne received praise from the English ambassadors who saw her, although they warned the King that she spoke no other language than her native German. This hardly bothered the enamoured King, who was eager to meet his new bride and started appointing her royal household. The ladies who served Jane Seymour now smoothly transferred to the newly established court of Anne of Cleves, who was making a slow journey amidst wintry rains and blizzards from Germany to England.

Anne of Cleves approached England through Calais, the last English outpost on French soil. There, she was greeted by a delegation of ladies and gentlemen and met Anne Basset's parents, Lord and Lady Lisle. The new Queen made a favourable impression on Lady Lisle, who immediately informed her daughter that Anne of Cleves was "good and gentle to serve and please". In a letter to her mother, the excited Anne Basset wrote about the atmosphere of anticipation generated by the new Queen's arrival to Calais:

"It shall be no little rejoicement to us, her Grace's servants here, that shall attend daily upon her, and most comfort to the King's majesty, whose highness is not a little desirous to have her Grace here".[6]

Anne's letter contains a curious remark. She thanked her mother for her precious advice touching "continuance in the King's favour".[7] The nature of this advice is unknown, but if Anne was indeed the King's mistress, her mother probably instructed her on how not to raise the Queen's suspicion and ingratiate herself with her new royal mistress. Lady Lisle wanted to use her daughter's influence with the King to secure a court appointment for another child of hers, Katherine Basset. Katherine was older than Anne but apparently not half

"Continuance in the King's favour"

as beautiful, and when Anne broached the subject of her sister's appointment, the King told her that he preferred "fair" ladies to serve his wife.[8] Lady Lisle was not easily discouraged and quizzed John Norris, one of the King's numerous gentlemen ushers, about the Queen's household and chief gentlewomen who could help her. She learned that among the ladies of Anne of Cleves's Privy Chamber were Eleanor Manners, Countess of Rutland, Alice Browne and Katherine Edgecombe. The Countess of Rutland was Lady Lisle's friend, and she employed Katherine Basset as her own maid so that the girl could accompany her to court.

The countess was an experienced lady-in-waiting; she was first recorded as Anne Boleyn's attendant in 1532 and retained her position as Jane Seymour's servant. Her husband, Thomas Manners, became Lord Chamberlain in Jane Seymour's household, and Lady Rutland enjoyed a high degree of privilege, often serving the Queen at table and having close access to her on a daily basis. On 17 February 1540, Lady Rutland wrote a kind letter to Lady Lisle wherein she informed her that she promised to "do the best I can do prefer her [Katherine Basset] here, for I would be right glad thereof, both of the great honesty that is in her".[9] She also advised Lady Lisle to approach Mother Lowe, who served as superintendent of Anne of Cleves's German maids and who had a close relationship with the Queen. Katherine Basset was very desirous to serve in the Queen's household and asked her mother to send Mother Lowe a "good token, that she might better remember me".[10]

While Lady Lisle actively campaigned to place her daughter in Anne of Cleves's household, a marital drama was unfolding behind closed doors. Although Henry VIII fell in love with Anne of Cleves's portrait, the woman herself failed to arouse similar feelings in the King when he saw her in the flesh. After their first meeting, Henry complained that his German bride was not as beautiful as his ambassadors reported. But there was no way out, and the King married Anne on 6 January 1540.

Their wedding night was a disaster. The King claimed that Anne failed to arouse him sexually because he judged her to be "no maid". Henry scrutinized every inch of his new wife's body, relaying intimate details of her anatomy to the members of his Privy Chamber afterwards. "The looseness of her breasts and other tokens" convinced the King that Anne of Cleves was not a virgin, and he conceived an apparent distaste for her physique.[11] On her part, the Queen appeared embarrassed to talk about what was going on in her bedchamber when the King visited her and had naively asked her ladies-in-waiting whether a kiss on the mouth was not enough to deem her marriage consummated and thus indissoluble. "Madam, there must be more than this, or it will be long ere we have a Duke

"Continuance in the King's favour"

of York, which all this realm most desired", was Lady Rutland's resolute reply.[12]

It seems that only Alice Browne, wife of the King's Master of the Horse and the chief gentlewoman in the Queen's Privy Chamber, was able to guess the real reason behind Henry VIII's decision to repudiate Anne of Cleves. The King and his wife had absolutely nothing in common. Henry liked vivacious, erudite women who sang, danced and read poetry. Anne could do none of these things. She was reportedly of "low and gentle conditions" and had been brought up in a sheltered manner by her strict mother. She passed her time mostly with needlework and could neither sing nor play an instrument "for they take it here in Germany for a rebuke and an occasion of lightness that great ladies should be learned or have any knowledge of music".[13] She also abstained from any sort of "merry cheer" and had no gambling skills.

Anne was apparently a quick learner and had the gift of endearing people to her. Nevertheless, when Lady Browne met Anne in Calais, she "she saw in the Queen such fashion and manner of bringing up so gross [unsuitable] that in her judgment the King should never heartily love her".[14] Additionally, when Anne met the King for the first time in early January 1540, she failed to recognize him when he approached her in disguise and planted a kiss on her lips. Their relationship was doomed from that point on because the

King took Anne's failure to recognize him as a slight to his honour. Had Anne read medieval romances, she would have known that this was a charade in a game of courtly love, but God-fearing maidens in her native Germany were not supposed to read chivalric romances. By the summer of 1540, Anne of Cleves's marriage to Henry VIII was dissolved, and the former Queen was from henceforward known as "the King's beloved sister". She received a large annuity and several manors in the countryside, including Anne Boleyn's family home at Hever. She was also allowed to retain her ladies-in-waiting and maids of honour.

Lady Lisle's suit to Mother Lowe was apparently successful, as her daughter Katherine was finally appointed as Anne of Cleves's maid. Katherine Basset's happiness was brief, however, because she soon had to leave the bustling court behind and accompany her royal mistress to rural retirement. She was recorded as one of "Anne of Cleves's women" in 1541.[15] It was during one of her stays at Hever Castle in Kent that Katherine met Henry Ashley, a local esquire whom she married on 8 December 1547.

Katherine's sister Anne was luckier because she stayed at court and retained her position within the royal household, but another young girl had taken her place in the King's affection. A newcomer to court, Katherine Howard, dazzled the King with her youthful charm. Mistress Howard was still in

"Continuance in the King's favour"

her teens when she was selected to join the ranks of Anne of Cleves's maids, and the King "did cast a fancy" to her immediately after her arrival.[16] She embodied everything the aging monarch valued in a woman; beauty, vivaciousness, wit and talent for courtly entertainments. Related to the leading noble of the court, Thomas Howard, third Duke of Norfolk, Katherine was also a good catch.

The ambitious Howards quickly took notice of the King's interest in one of their own. Katherine was suddenly worth investing in. Her step-grandmother, Agnes Howard, Dowager Duchess of Norfolk, in whose household Katherine had spent her formative years, showered the girl with new clothes and jewels. The old lady had also instructed her young charge how to behave and "in what sort to entertain the King's Highness and how often".[17]

Soon, the King's merry romps with Katherine under the Dowager Duchess of Norfolk's roof became notorious and reached the ears of Katherine Howard's childhood friend, Joan Bulmer. Joan decided to try her luck and appealed directly to Katherine for a post at court. In a letter she wrote two weeks before Katherine married the King, Joan hinted that she was privy to Katherine's secrets, and it would be wise if Mistress Howard, in her newfound happiness, remembered Joan's past services. Despite her young age, Katherine Howard had secrets she wished to remain hidden in her past. But her past

Great Ladies

came knocking at her door, and there was nothing she could do about it.

NOTES

[1] *Letters and Papers, Foreign and Domestic, Henry VIII,* Volume 14 Part 1, n. 144.

[2] *Letters and Papers, Foreign and Domestic, Henry VIII,* Volume 12 Part 2, n. 209.

[3] Muriel St Clare Byrne, *The Lisle Letters,* Volume 5, p. 616.

[4] Ibid., p. 615.

[5] *Letters and Papers, Foreign and Domestic, Henry VIII,* Volume 14 Part 2, n. 284.

[6] Ibid., n. 718.

[7] Ibid.

[8] Muriel St Clare Byrne, *The Lisle Letters,* Volume 6, p. 34.

[9] Ibid., p. 25.

[10] Ibid.

[11] H.A. Kelly, *The Matrimonial Trials of Henry VIII,* p. 270.

[12] Ibid.

[13] *Letters and Papers, Foreign and Domestic, Henry VIII,* Volume 14 Part 2, n. 33.

[14] *Letters and Papers, Foreign and Domestic, Henry VIII,* Volume 15, n.6.

[15] Nicolas Harris Nicholas, *Proceedings and Ordinances of the Privy Council of England,* Volume 7, p. 220.

[16] *Letters and Papers, Foreign and Domestic, Henry VIII,* Volume 16, n. 1409.

[17] Ibid.

CHAPTER 10
"IS NOT THE QUEEN ABED YET?"

Henry VIII married Katherine Howard on 28 July 1540 at Oatlands Palace in Surrey. It was a private ceremony with only a handful of witnesses present. That same day, one of Henry VIII's most faithful servants, Thomas Cromwell, was executed for meddling into the King's private affairs. It was Cromwell who insisted on the King's marriage with Anne of Cleves and who ignored the power of Henry VIII's feelings for Katherine Howard. Several years later, Stephen Gardiner, Bishop of Winchester, would warn his fellow councillors how dangerous it was to "take a share in marriages of princes", citing Cromwell, who was ruined by the failed Cleves match.[1]

Henry VIII's recent marital misadventure proved that he was interested in marrying women whose virginity was unquestionable. He believed that Katherine Howard, who might have been as young as sixteen at the time of her royal wedding, was innocent in the ways of the world. Yet Katherine, despite her young age, was not a virgin. While living in the Dowager Duchess of Norfolk's household, she was pestered by music teacher Henry Manox to let him touch her intimate parts, but Katherine refused to have full intercourse with him. Later on, she had a long-term sexual liaison with Francis Dereham, who served as a page in Agnes Howard's household. Other young girls who shared a dormitory with Katherine Howard would attest that there was "such puffing and blowing between them" that they had trouble sleeping.[2]

The dowager duchess was aware that the young couple was in love, but she would make light of the situation, and whenever Dereham was not around when she needed him, she joked that he was probably in Katherine Howard's chamber. Available evidence suggests that the dowager duchess had no idea that the relationship between Katherine and Dereham was sexual in nature, and when she had once walked in on them kissing, she slapped them both.

Katherine Howard made several female friends in the household of her step-grandmother. These young women now flooded the Queen with requests to give them posts in her newly forming household. Joan Bulmer, who often shared a bed with Katherine during the heady days of their youth, reminded the young Queen that she was her "secretary", i.e. privy to her secrets, and begged Katherine to recall her from her miserable life in the countryside. Joan was unsuccessful in her suit because her husband forbade her to leave his side.[3] Other ladies were more successful. Katherine Tilney, Margaret Benet, Alice Restwold and Malyn Tilney, all of whom knew

"Is not the Queen abed yet?"

Katherine before, received the posts of chamberers.[4] Katherine's reaction to seeing Alice Restwold reveals that the young Queen was happy to employ familiar faces. Alice later recalled that when she first came to Katherine, the Queen "kissed and welcomed her" offering a post of a chamberer. She also presented Alice with decorations for her French hood and gave her a tablet of gold to suspend from a girdle, a decorative cord worn around the waist.[5] It is highly revealing that the ladies who shared the same upbringing as Katherine Howard received the posts of chamberers, the lowest rank among the Queen's private servants. Chamberers performed menial tasks such as emptying chamber pots, making beds and sweeping the rooms. These tasks were still performed within the private royal suite, but they were deemed to be beneath the dignity of ladies-in-waiting and maids of honour, who came from the upper echelons of nobility.

There was early discord in Katherine Howard's household when one of her sisters was dismissed from her service and replaced by Jane Boleyn, Viscountess Rochford.[6] Brought up at court from an early age, Lady Rochford served as Katharine of Aragon's maid of honour and later transferred into the household of her sister-in-law, Anne Boleyn. After Anne's execution, Jane became a lady-in-waiting to Jane Seymour and later Anne of Cleves. In her late thirties, Lady Rochford was twice older than Katherine Howard and cut a

Great Ladies

rather sombre figure. She was described as a "widow in black", still mourning the tragic loss of her husband, George Boleyn.[7] For centuries, it has been assumed that Lady Rochford played a crucial part in the downfall of the Boleyns, but there is nothing in contemporary sources to suggest that she was the crown's star witness who accused her own husband.[8] After the executions, Jane smoothly transferred to the household of Jane Seymour and rode in the second chariot, a position of considerable privilege, at the Queen's funeral in November 1537. The fact that she had an intimate conversation with Anne of Cleves following the disastrous wedding night proves that she had a unique ability to ingratiate herself with her royal mistresses.

Jane Boleyn quickly gained Katherine Howard's trust and became her chief lady-in-waiting. When the young Queen renewed her relations with Thomas Culpeper, gentleman of the King's Privy Chamber, she informed him that he should pay her visits "when my Lady Rochford is here, for then I shall be best at leisure to be at your commandment".[9] Being married to the chronically ill Henry VIII must have been trying for a young and vivacious Katherine, whose name was linked with the dashing Culpeper when she first came to court as a maid of honour. The King's injured leg and large bulk did not permit him to indulge as frequently in physical pursuits such as hunting or jousting, so he whiled away his days at his desk

"Is not the Queen abed yet?"

or in bed, poring through paperwork and books. He was still able to ride, but long hours in the saddle were now only a distant memory. Henry's legs, covered with fistulas and ulcers, were a source of constant pain, and many believed that the King would soon die. If Katherine Howard felt any distaste for her much older, sickly husband, she cloaked it with a display of wifely obedience. There was "no other will but his", a motto she adopted upon becoming Queen and wore embroidered in gold thread around her sleeves.

The King, enamoured with Katherine, believed that he had acquired a "jewel of womanhood". Although no undisputable likeness of Katherine exists today, observers remarked that she possessed an "excellent beauty, in which she surpasses all the ladies in England".[10] Henry VIII took pleasure in displaying his new bride and spared no expense to enhance her appearance. "The King had no wife who made him spend so much money in dresses and jewels as she did", observers remarked.[11] Yet despite the privileges of her new position, the young Queen was becoming increasingly isolated at court.

In the spring of 1541, Katherine began showing considerable favour to Thomas Culpeper, showering him with gifts and messages carried by Lady Rochford. Culpeper was young and handsome, and he served in the King's Privy Chamber, where he worked on a daily basis, accompanying

Henry VIII wherever he went. The Queen's letter addressed to Culpeper when he was sick clearly points out that she had developed strong feelings for him. "I never longed so much for a thing as I do to see you and to speak with you", she wrote, adding that she wished he were with her to "see what pain I take in writing to you".[12]

According to the Queen's chamberers, Katherine Howard acted strangely during the summer progress of 1541. In early August at Lincoln, she spent two nights in Lady Rochford's lodgings and met Culpeper there. Katherine Tilney went to check up on the Queen and took Margaret Morton with her, but Katherine sent them to their rooms. While Tilney obediently went to bed, Morton stayed up late and returned to her quarters at two o'clock in the morning. "Jesus, is not the Queen abed yet?" Tilney asked. "Yes, even now", was Morton's resolute reply.[13] When the royal party arrived at Hatfield in late August, Morton observed the Queen looking out the window at Culpeper in a way "that she thought there was love between them".[14]

It is clear that when the Queen had her private nocturnal trysts with Culpeper, she did not like to be disturbed. When they met at Pontefract Castle, the Queen was angry with Margaret Morton and Mistress Lufkin, who came to check up on her, and "threatened to put them away", i.e. dismiss them. Morton believed that Lady Rochford "was the

"Is not the Queen abed yet?"

principal occasion of the Queen's folly" because Katherine Howard spent every night at Pontefract in Lady Rochford's chamber, with the door bolted from inside.[15] Despite these strange goings-on, it was not one of the Queen's ladies who gave away her secrets. Mary Hall, a young woman from Nottinghamshire who used to serve in the Dowager Duchess of Norfolk's household, told her brother, John Lascelles, that the Queen was "light both in living and conditions", divulging to him everything she knew about Katherine's youthful affairs with Manox and Dereham.[16] John Lascelles immediately informed Thomas Cranmer, Archbishop of Canterbury, and an investigation into Mary Hall's revelations was launched.

By the time Katherine Howard's past came to light in November 1541, the Queen had employed her former lover, Francis Dereham, as her secretary and usher. Dereham was apparently still in love with Katherine because he bragged about their past acquaintance. The Queen knew the risk such reckless boasting carried and paid Dereham for his silence, warning him to "take heed what words you speak".[17] During the interrogations of the Queen and her circle, Francis Dereham told the royal councillors that although he and Katherine had been lovers in the past, he was succeeded in her affection by Thomas Culpeper.

When the Queen's involvement with Culpeper leaked out, Katherine Howard blamed her chief lady-in-waiting for

Great Ladies

pestering her to grant Culpeper an audience. The Queen claimed that Lady Rochford told her that Culpeper "meant nothing but honesty". The Queen also said that she stood up to Lady Rochford and commanded her to "trouble her no more with such light matters".[18] Culpeper, on the other hand, blamed both the Queen and her lady-in-waiting, trying to depict himself as a victim of unbridled female lust. The Queen, Culpeper said, "was actually dying of love for his person", and Lady Rochford "provoked him much to love the Queen".[19] Despite these revelations, Thomas Culpeper and Katherine Howard both steadfastly maintained that there was nothing improper about their relationship. They claimed they had no sexual relations during their meetings, although Culpeper, somewhat recklessly, admitted that he intended to make love to Katherine. Lady Rochford's testimony was extraordinarily brief. She admitted to have helped the Queen in arranging trysts with Culpeper, but she either "heard or saw nothing of what passed" between the young couple or was asleep when they met in her chamber. In the end, Lady Rochford somewhat contradicted her earlier statement when she revealed that she believed that Culpeper had carnal knowledge of Katherine.[20]

On 13 November 1541, the Queen's household was dissolved. Sir Thomas Wriothesley, the King's secretary, came to Hampton Court to inform Katherine Howard's staff about what had happened. He gathered the Queen's ladies and other

"Is not the Queen abed yet?"

servants in the Great Chamber and "there openly afore them declared certain offences that she had done in misusing her body with certain persons afore the King's time".[21] The next day, 14 November, the Queen was conveyed by barge to the former Abbey of Syon, where she was kept "in the estate of a Queen" but with reduced staff. She had only a set of three chambers to occupy, together with her small household, and was now forbidden to dine under the cloth of estate or dress in luxurious clothes indicating her royal status. The King had graciously allowed Katherine to pick her favourite ladies: four gentlewomen and two chamberers. One of them was Isabella Baynton, the Queen's sister and wife of Sir Edward Baynton, who served as vice-chamberlain of the Queen's household. That same day, 14 November 1541, Lady Rochford, Francis Dereham and Thomas Culpeper were taken by barge to the Tower of London. With their goods and chattels inventoried, there was little chance that they would walk free again.

After her banishment from court, Katherine Howard found herself on the verge of a nervous breakdown: "She would neither eat nor drink since this matter was known, but intended to kill herself." The precaution was taken to remove sharp objects such as knives "and all such things as wherewith she might hurt herself".[22] The mental health of Katherine's lady-in-waiting, Lady Rochford, was also fragile. The imperial ambassador Chapuys reported that three days after her

Great Ladies

imprisonment, on 17 November 1541, Lady Rochford "had been seized with a fit of madness".[23] Henry VIII appointed his own physician to treat her and placed her under the care of Lady Anne Russell, wife of Lord Admiral John Russell, Earl of Bedford. Why Lady Russell was chosen as Lady Rochford's hostess remains unclear. Perhaps the two women were known to have been friends, although it appears that the Russells were highly esteemed by the King, who had sent his own physician to the Lord Admiral when he was dangerously ill in 1538.

Thomas Culpeper and Francis Dereham were executed on 10 December 1541 at the Tower Green. After "exhortation made to the people to pray for him", Culpeper kneeled down and was beheaded with an axe. Culpeper had long been one of the King's favourites, and he persistently maintained until the end that he and Katherine Howard were not lovers in the carnal sense. Henry VIII had thus commuted his sentence to a mere beheading. Francis Dereham, on the other hand, was to experience the full horror of being "hanged, dismembered, disembowelled, beheaded and quartered", all for having a relationship with a young woman who later became the King of England's wife.[24]

When Katherine Howard was rowed from Syon Abbey to the Tower on 10 February 1542, the stark reality hit her hard as she passed by the decapitated heads of Thomas

"Is not the Queen abed yet?"

Culpeper and Francis Dereham that had been left rotting on a spike above London Bridge. At that moment, she realized there was no hope for her. When informed about her impending execution, the young woman asked that a wooden block should be brought to her chamber so that she could practice how to put her head on it. It was a reasonable request: Katherine had certainly heard that an inexperienced executioner could hack her head and shoulders to pieces and painfully injure her before striking the final blow, and she wanted to be prepared.

The Queen's lady-in-waiting, "that bawd, Lady Rochford", as her indictment condemned her, was rowed back from Lady Russell's house to the Tower on 9 February 1542.[25] The imperial ambassador heard that she had regained her senses when she learned that she would die regardless of whether she was insane or not. The King was so eager to send her to the scaffold "as an example and warning to others" that he had passed a special law allowing him to execute an insane person.[26]

On the crisp wintry morning of 13 February 1542, Katherine Howard made her way to the wooden scaffold erected on the spot where, six years earlier, her cousin Anne Boleyn had been executed for adultery. The young Queen was "so weak that she could hardly speak" and kept her speech brief.[27] When the executioner performed his task, Lady

Great Ladies

Rochford approached the scaffold and had to put her head down on the wooden block where her royal mistress had lost her life only minutes before. An eyewitness recorded that both Katherine Howard and Jane Boleyn "made the most godly and Christians' end that ever was heard tell of (I think) since the world's creation".[28] They confessed their guilt and asked the gathered crowd to pray for Henry VIII's wealth and prosperity.

The King who sent his second wife to the scaffold was deeply hurt by his young wife's betrayal, but after a brief period of heartache and tears, he brazened it out by demonstrating that he was not affected at all. On one occasion, he banqueted with twenty-six ladies sitting at his table and thirty-five at another one located close by. Among the young women whom he showed especial attention was Anne Basset. When Katherine Howard's maids of honour had been dismissed in November 1541, Mistress Basset stayed at court, where the King obliged himself to provide for her. Speculation was rife that the King's next wife would be one of Katherine Howard's young servants, although the imperial ambassador bitingly remarked that "there are few, if any, ladies at court nowadays likely to aspire to the honour of becoming one of the King's wives".[29] Becoming Henry VIII's next wife would be like stepping into the lion's den.

"Is not the Queen abed yet?"

NOTES

[1] John Schofield, *Thomas Cromwell*, p. 402.

[2] Sir Harris Nicolas, *Proceedings and Ordinances of the Privy Council of England*, Volume, p. 352.

[3] Josephine Wilkinson, *Katherine Howard: The Tragic Story of Henry VIII's Fifth Queen*, p. 145.

[4] *Letters and Papers, Foreign and Domestic, Henry VIII*, Volume 15, n. 21.

[5] *Letters and Papers, Foreign and Domestic, Henry VIII*, Volume 16, n. 1339.

[6] Ibid., n. 1366. Katherine Howard's recent biographer identifies the sister as Mary Howard, who married Sir Edmund Trafford. Josephine Wilkinson, *Katherine Howard: The Tragic Story of Henry VIII's Fifth Queen*, Kindle edition.

[7] Elizabeth Norton, *The Boleyn Women*, p. 193.

[8] As demonstrated by Julia Fox in her groundbreaking biography *Jane Boleyn: The Infamous Lady Rochford* (Phoenix, 2008).

[9] TNA SP 1/167/14: Katherine Howard's letter to Thomas Culpeper.

[10] M. Jean Kaulek, *Correspondance Politique de MM. de Castillon et de Marillac*, p. 363.

[11] *Chronicle of King Henry VIII* (*The Spanish Chronicle*), p. 77.

[12] TNA SP 1/167/14, op. cit.

[13] *Letters and Papers, Foreign and Domestic, Henry VIII*, Volume 16, n. 1337.

[14] Ibid., n. 1338.

[15] Ibid.

[16] Ibid., n. 1334.

[17] Ibid., n. 1339.

[18] Examination of Queen Katherine Howard (*Calendar of the Manuscripts of the Marquis of Bath*, Volume 2, p. 10)

[19] *Letters and Papers, Foreign and Domestic, Henry VIII*, Volume 16, op.cit.

[20] Ibid.

[21] *Wriothesley's Chronicle*, Volume 1, pp. 130-131.

[22] *State Papers, King Henry the Eighth*, Volume 8 Part 5, p. 636.

[23] *Calendar of State Papers, Spain*, Volume 6 Part 1, n. 209.

[24] *Wriothesley's Chronicle*, Volume 1, p. 132.

[25] Ibid.

[26] *Calendar of State Papers, Spain*, Volume 6 Part 1, n. 209.

[27] *Letters and Papers, Foreign and Domestic, Henry VIII*, Volume 17, n. 100.

[28] Ibid., n. 106.

[29] *Calendar of State Papers, Spain,* Volume 6 Part 1, n. 232.

CHAPTER 11
"PRIVY TO ALL HER DOINGS"

Within a year of Katherine Howard's execution, Henry VIII was courting a lady of the same name but of much different disposition. Some people speculated that the ageing King was weary of "taking young wives" and this was why he had cast an appreciative eye on Katherine Parr, a twice-widowed lady in her early thirties.[1] Despite being much older than her executed predecessor, Katherine was a good-looking woman with a willowy figure and an immaculate sense of fashion. She was an exceptionally well-educated noblewoman and had a reputation of being intelligent, kind and pious. When Henry VIII married Katherine Parr, he was already fifty-two years old, and the new Queen was childless despite having been twice married before. This led some observers to conclude that this marriage would not produce children. The imperial ambassador Chapuys wrote that Katherine Parr was barren and less beautiful than Anne of Cleves, Henry's fourth wife, for whom the King conceived such strong distaste he divorced her within six months after marrying her. Yet Henry VIII found Katherine Parr's appearance attractive and her company stimulating and allowed her a great degree of freedom in her courtly activities.

Becoming Queen of England was a huge social advancement for a gentlewoman who led her life mostly in rural settings taking care of her incapacitated husbands and two of her stepchildren, and Katherine Parr took her new role seriously and enthusiastically. Before she married Henry VIII, she already had a suitor in the person of Thomas Seymour, younger brother of the late Queen Jane. Yet Katherine could not refuse the King's advances and had to accept his suit, setting her own desires aside. Like most people of her epoch, Katherine saw the occurrences in her life as providential and later wrote to Thomas explaining why she decided to marry the King:

"As truly as God is God, my mind was fully bent, the other time I was at liberty, to marry you before any man I knew. Howbeit, God withstood my will therein most vehemently for a time, and, through His grace and goodness, made that possible which seemed to me most impossible— that was, made me to renounce utterly mine own will, and to follow His will most willingly."[2]

Because Katherine saw her new role as one given to her by God himself, she decided to use her newfound power and influence to spread his word at court. Her household soon

"Privy to all her doings"

became a centre of learned religious discussions. John Foxe, the author of *Book of Martyrs,* wrote that the Queen was "much given to the reading and study of the Holy Scriptures" and that every day in the afternoon she held regular meetings with her chaplains, ladies-in-waiting and "others that were disposed to hear". The Queen would serve refreshments in her Privy Chamber and listen to hour-long sermons that were followed by enlivened discussions about "such abuses as in the church then were rife".[3] These meetings were by no means secretive, and Henry VIII knew very well what his wife was doing in her spare time. Katherine often initiated heated debates about religion and thrived when her royal husband gave ear to her opinions. What the Queen did not know was that the King was growing irritated by her commanding tone and lack of deference to his judgment. In February 1546, the new imperial ambassador, François van der Delft, reported that there was rumour "about the new Queen". The ambassador did not know the origin of or reason for such a rumour since the King "showed no alteration in his demeanour" towards Katherine Parr, but some people attributed it to the fact that Katherine appeared to have been barren.[4] "Madame Suffolk is much talked about and in great favour", the ambassador wrote, hinting that she may have been a potential candidate for the King's next wife.[5] This Madame Suffolk was Katherine Parr's friend and lady-in-waiting, Katherine Brandon, Duchess of Suffolk. She was a daughter of Maria de Salinas, Lady Willoughby, Katharine of Aragon's faithful Spanish servant. She married Charles Brandon, Duke of Suffolk, in 1533 when she was fourteen years old. Suffolk was Henry VIII's close friend and companion. Their friendship started before the King's accession in 1509 and ended with Suffolk's death in 1545. Katherine Brandon and Katherine Parr became close friends as well, with the duchess attending the Queen both in private and in public.

Almost immediately after Katherine Parr's wedding, the ranks of ladies-in-waiting were reformed. The Queen's sister, Anne Herbert, was promoted to the position of chief gentlewoman of the Privy Chamber, controlling access to the Queen and selecting those who were allowed to approach her. Anne Herbert was not a newcomer to court; she served as lady-in-waiting to her sister's executed predecessor and received Katherine Howard's jewels for safekeeping in November 1541.[6] It is often stated that Anne served all of Henry VIII's six wives, but her name started to crop up in the records no earlier than during Jane Seymour's time as Queen in 1537.[7]

Anne married William Herbert, a trusted servant of Henry VIII's, at some point in 1537. There is a hint that she might have had an extramarital relationship with the executed Thomas Culpeper in the early 1540s. During one of their

"Privy to all her doings"

clandestine meetings in 1541, Queen Katherine Howard reproached Culpeper for sleeping around, saying: "I marvel that you could so much dissemble as to say that you loved me so openly and yet would and did so soon lie with another, called Anne Herbert".[8] A further exchange between them reveals that Katherine Howard was well oriented in the love affairs of members of the Parr family because she cited William Parr's extramarital relationship with one Dorothy Bray, telling Culpeper defiantly that if she wanted, she could have brought him "into as good a trade as Bray hath my lord Parr in".[9]

William, brother of Katherine Parr and Anne Herbert, was famous for his marital misadventures. His arranged marriage to Anne Bourchier was never a happy one, and in 1541 Anne eloped with her lover, with whom she soon had a child. Bourchier's child was declared illegitimate, and William fell in love with Elisabeth Brooke, a young and beautiful maid of honour who served at court. But whereas the law allowed William Parr to separate from his adulterous wife, it did not allow him to divorce her and remarry. His only chance at happiness with Elisabeth Brooke was to wait until the death of his first wife because only Anne Bourchier's death could create a legal foundation for his remarriage.

Despite these scandals in her immediate family, Katherine Parr's reputation remained unscathed. She chose

Great Ladies

her ladies-in-waiting with admirable prudence and integrity, honouring those who served at court for years but also using her prerogative to employ new ones. The Queen's sister was not the only kinswoman who entered the ranks of Katherine Parr's ladies-in-waiting. The widowed Lady Maud Lane was Katherine's much favoured first cousin, who entered her household in 1543, together with her parents: Sir William Parr, Baron Parr of Horton, who became the Queen's chamberlain, and Mary Parr, who became the Queen's lady-in-waiting. Whereas Lady Lane served daily at court and shared Katherine's religious zeal, it is less clear what duties Lady Lane's mother had and whether she was at constant attendance on the Queen. Mary Parr's name appears in the Queen's household list only once, the occasion being Henry VIII's funeral in 1547.

Another noblewoman related to the Queen who received a coveted employment at court was Katherine Parr's stepdaughter, sixteen-year-old Margaret Neville. Having no child of her own, Katherine Parr raised Margaret as her daughter over the course of her marriage to John Neville, Baron Latimer, and the two shared a close relationship. Henry VIII married Katherine Parr within months of her second husband's death, cutting her widowhood short, and the early payments of the Queen show that she supplied Margaret with a set of new mourning clothes. The Queen took full advantage

"Privy to all her doings"

of her new position and provided the best education for Margaret. "I am never able to render to Her Grace sufficient thanks for the goodly education and tender love and bountiful goodness which I have ever more found in her Highness", Margaret wrote about Katherine Parr in her last will.[10] She died at the age of nineteen in 1546.

Throughout Katherine Parr's time as Henry VIII's wife, religious divisions within the court were palpable and very dangerous, as the Queen was to experience on her own. The court was now divided into two factions: Catholic and Protestant. The Catholics were led by Stephen Gardiner, Bishop of Winchester, who was eager to purge the King's circle of "heretics", people who dared to question the Church doctrine and read the Bible for themselves. The evangelicals within the Privy Council assumed an increasingly important role on the political and religious front, several of them being Henry VIII's closest friends and advisers. "The King favours these stirrers of heresy, the Earl of Hertford [Edward Seymour] and Lord Admiral [John Dudley, Viscount Lisle]", wrote the indignant imperial ambassador, adding that he suspected this was because "the Queen, instigated by the Duchess of Suffolk, Countess of Hertford and the Admiral's wife, shows herself infected".[11]

The three women named in this dispatch—Katherine Brandon, Duchess of Suffolk; Anne Seymour, Countess of

Great Ladies

Hertford; and Jane Dudley, Viscountess Lisle—were closely associated with Katherine Parr. They were also known for their religious zeal, close relationships with their husbands and biting wits. It was well known at court that the Queen hosted religious gatherings in her private chambers and often debated religious matters with her ladies, chaplains and with the King himself. It was too much to bear for the Catholics at court, especially for Stephen Gardiner, who decided to strike. The gossip about a new Queen mentioned earlier in this chapter was part of Gardiner's whispering campaign against Katherine Parr; they aimed at decreasing the Queen's confidence and reminding her that she was, like all of Henry VIII's previous wives, expendable. Yet Katherine believed that the King, who continued to show her his goodwill in private and in public, would protect her from the oncoming maelstrom of intrigue.

At some point in 1546, a young gentlewoman, Anne Askew, was arrested and questioned about her seditious religious views. She was very vocal in expressing them, and it was believed that she had friends among Katherine Parr's ladies-in-waiting. Gardiner hoped that Askew would break under interrogation and implicate the Queen and her ladies, but she did not. Brutally tortured by Thomas Wriothesley and Richard Rich, Anne later testified that "they did put me on the rack because I confessed no ladies or gentlemen to be of my

"Privy to all her doings"

opinion".[12] It is apparent that she was protecting her high-profile sponsors, such as Anne Seymour, Countess of Hertford, and Joan Denny, wife of Sir Anthony Denny, Henry VIII's Groom of the Stool and personal favourite. These two women not only shared Anne's religious beliefs but sent her money while she was imprisoned in the Tower. Yet Anne did not buckle under pressure and refused to implicate anyone. She was burned at the stake on 16 July 1546. Maimed and in pain after the inhumane torture sessions that sent shockwaves across the country, she had to be carried in a chair to her execution.

This was not the end of the Queen's trouble. Attacking Katherine Parr directly was too risky a move, even for such a powerful individual as Stephen Gardiner, so the bishop decided to attack her close ladies-in-waiting first. Three ladies were selected to be arrested and thoroughly interrogated about the activities in the Queen's private chambers, and their coffers and chests were searched for banned heretical books. These three ladies were Anne Herbert, Maud Lane and Elizabeth Tyrwhitt, who were "privy to all her doings" and much favoured by the Queen.[13] Yet this plan failed, and Gardiner had to find another way to accuse the Queen of heresy. Sensing that the King was becoming annoyed by his wife's enthusiastic religious rants, Gardiner decided to strike.

Great Ladies

An arrest warrant miraculously found its way to the Queen's chambers, and Katherine Parr had no other option but to approach her royal husband and plead for her life. Immediately upon learning that she was in danger, she commanded her ladies-in-waiting to remove their forbidden books. Then, as the evening approached, she took her sister, Anne Herbert, and cousin, Maud Lane, who carried a candle before the Queen, and visited the King in his bedchamber at Whitehall Palace. By the late 1540s, Henry VIII's health had deteriorated so much that he rarely ventured out of his private sanctum. He was increasingly dependent on a small group of trusted men who took care of his needs, dressing his ulcerous leg and helping him in everyday tasks. That evening the King was not alone, but surrounded by gentlemen who came for a late-night session of talking and merriment. Henry welcomed his wife warmly and immediately began to discuss religion. Katherine refused to take the bait. She sat on her husband's lap and told him that she would not dare to express her opinions because she was but a "silly poor woman, so much inferior in all respects of nature" to her wise royal husband. This was music to Henry's ears, but he was not easily pacified. "Not so, by St Mary", he replied, shaking his head, "you are become a doctor, Kate, to instruct us, as we take it, and not to be instructed or directed by us". Katherine then expatiated on the inferiority of women to men, adding that she talked about religion to divert the King and make him forget about his

"Privy to all her doings"

painful infirmities and to learn from him. The King was satisfied with her explanations and reassured her that they were "perfect friends" again. The next day, when Thomas Wriothesley came to arrest her, the King cursed at him violently and sent him away.[14] The Queen and her ladies were saved.

Henry VIII doted on Katherine Parr during his declining years. He showered her with jewels imported from abroad, expensive furs and clothes cut in the newest European fashions. The ageing King showed his sixth wife much favour and restored her to the position of a beloved wife and stepmother. He recognized her steadying influence on himself and on his three children, who craved motherly affection. "When I was at court with the King", wrote Henry VIII's son, Prince Edward, "you conferred on me so many kindnesses that I can scarcely grasp them with my mind".[15] The Queen was well aware that cultivating the good graces of her young stepson was crucial if she wanted to establish herself at court during his approaching reign. Katherine knew that her husband's health was deteriorating and that he would die soon, leaving Edward to succeed him as a minor, and she hoped to become Edward's regent. For the time being, however, the Queen concentrated on the royal family and her own household.

Great Ladies

The list of Katherine Parr's ladies-in-waiting for May 1546 shows that Henry VIII's daughters, Mary and Elizabeth, were "ordinary" members of the Queen's household, meaning that they served at court on a daily basis.[16] In 1544, Henry VIII decided to include Mary and Elizabeth in the new Act of Succession. They were still deemed as his illegitimate daughters—they never recovered the title of princess during their father's reign—but their royal status was confirmed. To celebrate the new act and memorialize his daughters' glorious restoration to the line of succession, Henry VIII commissioned the famous Whitehall family group portrait. The portrait captures the royal family in a private setting, with the King sitting in the centre beneath a canopy of state, flanked by his son and heir, Edward, on the left and his third wife, the late Jane Seymour, on the right. The King's hand rests firmly on Edward's shoulder, showing quite literally that Henry VIII's dynastic hopes now rested on the shoulders of a single surviving son. The inclusion of Jane Seymour rather than Katherine Parr showed that Henry VIII desired Jane to be regarded as the matriarch of the Tudor dynasty. Mary and Elizabeth stand on the opposing sides: Mary on the left and Elizabeth on the right. Their positions in the painting—so far from Henry VIII, Prince Edward and Jane Seymour, who took centre stage—show that their chances of inheriting the throne were deemed as slight.

"Privy to all her doings"

From 1544 until Henry VIII's death, Mary and Elizabeth were frequent visitors to court. In November 1545, prior to his daughters' visit, the King issued a warrant to the Great Wardrobe to deliver "stuff and apparel" for Mary, Elizabeth and their ladies-in-waiting.[17] The Queen often exchanged correspondence with both, but it seems that it was the younger Elizabeth who became her favourite.

By late 1546, Henry VIII had withdrawn from court and shut himself away at Whitehall Palace with his most trusted servants. Katherine Parr, the royal children and the entire court moved to Greenwich for the Christmas season, raising speculation among foreign ambassadors. The Queen had never left her husband "on a solemn occasion", and the imperial ambassador Van der Delft suspected that something was amiss.[18] Katherine now began to suspect that she might never see Henry VIII alive again, and that Christmas she gave Prince Edward a double portrait of herself and the King, hoping to stay in the young heir's remembrance. Katherine had a good reason to suspect that her royal husband was dying since she was kept away from him. "Neither the Queen nor the Lady Mary could see him, nor do we know that they will now do so", wrote Van der Delft on 10 January 1547, adding that there was a "great reason to conjecture that, whatever his health, it can only be bad and will not last long".[19] After the Christmas festivities, Katherine Parr moved from

Great Ladies

Greenwich to Westminster, but she was still denied an audience with the dying Henry VIII.

Although Henry's death was obviously imminent, his own physicians were afraid to tell him he was dying because they could be arrested for treason under the Treason Act by predicting the death of a King. It was Sir Anthony Denny, the King's Groom of the Stool, who told the dying monarch that "in man's judgment you are not like to live", urging him to call for a confessor. The King believed that "the mercy of God is able to pardon me all my sins, yes, though they were greater than they be". Still, Henry was not in a hurry to call for a priest. Denny asked if the King would like to see "any learned man to confer withal and open his mind unto". Henry nodded and said: "If I had any, it should be Dr Cranmer, but I will first take a little sleep. And then, as I feel myself, I will advise you upon the matter."

By the time Archbishop Thomas Cranmer was summoned, the King had lost the power of speech. Cranmer urged Henry to give him some sort of a sign that he put his trust in Christ's mercy; when the archbishop held the dying King's hand in his, the King suddenly "wring it as hard as he could".[20] Cranmer and all those who encircled the King's bed took it as a sign that Henry VIII died in the faith of Christ. The King expired on 28 January 1547 at about two o'clock in the morning and passed from history straight into legend.

"Privy to all her doings"

NOTES

[1] *Chronicle of King Henry VIII* (*The Spanish Chronicle*), p. 107.

[2] Janel Mueller, *Katherine Parr: Complete Works and Correspondence*, p. 382.

[3] John Foxe, *The Actes and Monuments of John Foxe*, Volume 5, p. 554.

[4] *Letters and Papers, Foreign and Domestic, Henry VIII*, Volume 12 Part 1, n. 289.

[5] Ibid.

[6] *Letters and Papers, Foreign and Domestic, Henry VIII*, Volume 16, n. 1389.

[7] Muriel St Clare Byrne, *The Lisle Letters*, Volume 4, p. 147.

[8] Josephine Wilkinson, *Katherine Howard: The Tragic Story of Henry VIII's Fifth Queen*, Kindle edition.

[9] Ibid.

[10] The last will of Margaret Neville, TNA, PROB 11, quoted in Susan James, *Catherine Parr: Henry VIII's Last Love*, p. 118.

[11] *Letters and Papers, Foreign and Domestic, Henry VIII*, Volume 21 Part 2, n. 756.

[12] Christopher Anderson, *The Annals of the English Bible*, Volume 2, p. 196.

[13] John Foxe, *The Actes and Monuments of John Foxe*, Volume 5, p. 554.

[14] Ibid.

[15] Janel Mueller, *Katherine Parr: Complete Works and Correspondence*, p. 121.

[16] *Letters and Papers, Foreign and Domestic, Henry VIII*, Volume 12 Part 1, n. 969.

[17] *Letters and Papers, Foreign and Domestic, Henry VIII*, Volume 12 Part 2, n. 909.

[18] Ibid., n. 605.

[19] Ibid., n. 684.

[20] J. J. Scarisbrick, *Henry VIII*, pp. 495-96.

CHAPTER 12
"A SECOND COURT"

Henry VIII's death and his son's accession heralded a new dawn for Katherine Parr and the women at court. The nine-year-old Prince Edward, now King Edward VI, was too young to rule in his own right, and Henry VIII had made necessary provisions for his son's guidance and government in the last weeks of his life. He designated that sixteen executors of his last will would constitute a Council of Regency, with twelve other advisors. The old King made it luminously clear that he wanted decisions to be taken by a majority vote and that there would be no one individual who would have pre-eminence over the others.

Yet Henry VIII's last will was thwarted immediately after his death. Edward Seymour, Earl of Hertford and the young King's maternal uncle, became Lord Protector of England and the Duke of Somerset. The dukedom of Somerset was linked to the royal family: it was borne by Henry VII's Beaufort ancestors and later conferred on this King's youngest son, Edmund, who died in his early childhood. Henry VIII revived this title by conferring the double dukedoms of Richmond and Somerset onto his illegitimate son, Henry Fitzroy, who died in 1536.

"A second court"

The appointment of Edward Seymour as Lord Protector was a blow to Katherine Parr, who had begun signing her letters as "Kateryn the Quene Regente KP" in anticipation of becoming a regent herself. It was not an unrealistic expectation on the Queen's part since she had been appointed Regent of England during Henry VIII's absence due to the war in France in 1544, and sixteenth-century Europe saw an explosion of female rulers. Yet Henry VIII's last will made it clear that he did not envisage Katherine as regent during Edward VI's minority. Effectively robbed of her chance to exert political influence in the newly formed regime, Katherine Parr now decided to concentrate on her private life. Thomas Seymour, the dashing younger brother of the Lord Protector, renewed his suit and proposed to Katherine immediately after Henry VIII's death. Katherine was torn between duty and her own desires. As a royal widow, she was expected to wait at least two years before marrying again, but Thomas urged her "to change the two years into two months".[1] The thirty-five-year-old Dowager Queen was a passionate woman, and she soon embarked on a secret love affair with Seymour, inviting him to her manor house at Chelsea late at night on several occasions. It is clear from their passionate love letters that before their secret wedding took place in the spring of 1547, they entered into a fully binding marriage pre-contract sealed with consummation that rendered their relationship legally indissoluble.[2]

Katherine Parr's hasty decision to remarry incurred public opprobrium and dismay. The Dowager Queen was condemned in strong terms because many believed that since she was suspected to have been barren, she took Thomas Seymour as husband to fulfil her repressed sexual desires. Even Katherine's "assured loving friend", the Duchess of Suffolk, mocked the couple, suggestively naming a stallion and a mare in her stables "Seymour" and "Parr".[3]

Some people at court, like Katherine Parr's former lady-in-waiting Anne Seymour, newly created Duchess of Somerset, saw the Dowager Queen's mésalliance as debasing her royal dignity. Without a Queen consort at Edward VI's side, both Katherine Parr and Anne Seymour fought for precedence at court. A contemporary *Chronicle of King Henry VIII*, known also as *The Spanish Chronicle*, depicts their feud in vivid detail, perhaps too vividly to take it at face value. The chronicle ascribed the fierce rivalry between the Seymour brothers to the discord between their wives. The chronicle goes on to say that since Edward Seymour was Lord Protector and "ruled the kingdom", his wife believed that "she ought to be more considered than the Queen, and claimed to take precedence of her". There is even an example of how Anne Seymour had "thrust herself forward, and sat in the Queen's place" during one of the Masses in the royal chapel. The chronicle says that Anne's rudeness towards Katherine

"A second court"

brought about the Queen Dowager's premature death; "she fell ill, and in a short time died".[4] This source does not mention the real cause of Katherine Parr's death—childbed fever—and, although the story of the battle for precedence has been passed down by subsequent writers and embellished in the process, modern historians wisely treat it with a touch of reserve.

However, although *The Spanish Chronicle* often plays fast and loose with the facts, it is a mistake to dismiss the quarrel altogether.[5] There is a hint that the quarrel between Katherine Parr and Anne Seymour had indeed taken place. When the Dowager Queen gave birth to a daughter on 30 August 1548, Thomas Seymour mused that "it would be strange to some when his daughter came of age, taking [her] place above [the Duchess of Somerset], as a Queen's daughter".[6] These words strongly indicate that some sort of a power struggle occurred between the Dowager Queen and her former lady-in-waiting.

There certainly was no love lost between Katherine Parr and Anne Seymour. The Dowager Queen's seemingly warm relationship with Anne and Edward disintegrated after the Seymours became prominent at court following Henry VIII's death. Katherine was further disenchanted with Edward Seymour when he began granting leases on her dower lands without her approval and refused to restore her jewels. The jewels were an especially delicate subject with Katherine since they included pieces she received from Henry VIII as gifts, such as her wedding ring and a crown-headed brooch, and her personal property, such as the jewellery her mother willed to her in 1531. These valuables were left in the Tower for safekeeping after Henry VIII's death. Depriving the Dowager Queen of her rightful property would not be the only act of covetousness on the part of the Duke and Duchess of Somerset; in 1549, Anne and her brother were seen smuggling some fine fabrics from the royal silk house at Westminster.[7] Anne and her husband had no intention of honouring Katherine Parr's status as Henry VIII's widow and were offended when she married Thomas Seymour. "What cause have they to fear [you] having such a wife?" Katherine mused in one of her letters to Thomas.[8]

One reason why the Duchess of Somerset was reluctant to accept Katherine Parr's marriage to Thomas Seymour was that she saw the Dowager Queen as a rival. Soon after her marriage to Thomas became public knowledge, Katherine began to assemble her household. There was a question of how her status was to be defined since she had committed a mésalliance by marrying her social inferior. Yet Katherine Parr was not the only royal woman in England who married beneath her rank and retained her status. Henry VIII's younger sister, Mary Tudor, had famously married Charles

"A second court"

Brandon, Duke of Suffolk, but she had never relinquished her status as Queen of France. Many women acted similarly, and Katherine Parr still regarded herself as Dowager Queen.

Thomas Seymour was especially keen to emphasize that he married into the highest echelon of nobility and was eager to maintain his wife's "princely royalty". Katherine soon had a large court with 120 servants, including "the gentlewomen of the Queen's Highness's Privy Chamber . . . and also the maids which waited at large and other women being about her Grace".[9] Nobility still flocked to Katherine's new establishment that was termed "a second court" and rivalled the household of the Duke and Duchess of Somerset.[10]

At some point in 1547, Katherine Parr took Henry VIII's younger daughter, Elizabeth, into her household. At fourteen, Elizabeth was deemed too young to have a household of her own, so the decision was made that she would join the establishment of her much-loved royal stepmother. But instead of a safe haven, Katherine Parr's household became the stage of one of the most dramatic events of Elizabeth's life. When Thomas Seymour moved in with Katherine Parr after their clandestine wedding, Elizabeth saw him on a daily basis. Historical evidence strongly suggests that Seymour acted seductively towards Elizabeth, who at first found his attentions flattering, if embarrassing. Elizabeth often selected Thomas Seymour as her dancing partner, but then "she would laugh and pale at it". It is likely that Elizabeth didn't fully understand the implications of such behaviour, or, what's more plausible, she thought it innocent and harmless. But these innocent games encouraged Seymour to pursue Elizabeth more aggressively. He made it his habit to visit Elizabeth's bedchamber before she was out of bed, wishing her "good morrow and ask how she did, or strike her upon the back". If he found her still in bed, Seymour would draw back the bed curtains, bid her "good morrow" and "make as though he would come at her". Seymour often came to Elizabeth's bedchamber dressed only in his nightgown "bare legged and in his slippers", but he usually found her reading a book. It seems as though Elizabeth made it her habit to rise early in order to be dressed before Seymour's visitation.[11] Elizabeth's governess, Kat Ashley, chastised Seymour and told him that "it was an unseemly sight to come so bare legged to a maiden's chamber".[12]

The implication of invading a virgin's private space like that held a dangerous sexual undertone. During the Tudor period, men made a show of their muscular legs by wearing tight, leg-hugging stockings beneath their knee-length tunics. Legs and knees often symbolised the most intimate, hidden parts of one's body. Even marriages were symbolically consummated when the bare leg of a woman was touched by a man's bare foot; it was so common that a famous Tudor

"A second court"

proverb said that "there belonged more to a marriage than two pairs of bare legs".[13] In any case, Kat Ashley told Katherine Parr about Seymour's behaviour, but the Dowager Queen "made a small matter of it" and volunteered to visit Elizabeth's bedchamber with Seymour—and they did so together, adding more awkwardness to the situation. On one occasion, when the Dowager Queen was walking with Elizabeth in the gardens at Hanworth, Seymour approached Elizabeth and "cut her gown in a hundred pieces" while Katherine held her back.[14]

Whereas Katherine Parr saw nothing untoward in her husband's strange behaviour towards her stepdaughter, others found it downright scandalous. Details of Thomas Seymour's habits soon spread across the country and reached the capital. Anne Seymour, Duchess of Somerset, was shocked at the lack of discipline in Katherine Parr's household. She blamed Elizabeth's wayward governess, Kat Ashley, for allowing Seymour to dally with Henry VIII's daughter and took it upon herself to berate Kat in very strong terms. Anne rebuked Kat for allowing Elizabeth to travel by barge on the Thames late at night and for other "light parts". The duchess told Kat that "she was not worthy to have the governance of a King's daughter" and that she was too great a friend of Thomas Seymour.[15] These criticisms made little impression on Kat, who shrugged them off as nonsense. Yet in 1548, Thomas Seymour again overstepped the bounds of propriety, this time with Elizabeth's consent. Katherine Parr walked in on them when they were all alone while Seymour held Elizabeth in his arms. This was too much to bear for Katherine, who berated them both and decided to send Elizabeth away from her household. The Dowager Queen was pregnant at the time and wanted no distractions. Yet despite the difficult circumstances of their parting, Katherine Parr kept in touch with Elizabeth through mutual correspondence. In her letter written on 31 July 1548, Elizabeth expressed her worries about Katherine's health. The Dowager Queen was now thirty-six, "past middle age" by the standards of her epoch.[16] To become pregnant at this stage in life was deemed very dangerous, especially if it was a first pregnancy. Katherine suffered from morning sickness that persisted well into her eighth month and was "so sickly" that she could scarcely write back to Elizabeth.[17] In the summer of 1548, she moved to Sudeley Castle, a tranquil and picturesque place where the Dowager Queen wanted to establish her birthing chamber.

That summer Anne Seymour was also expecting a child. The Duchess of Somerset was about two years older than the Dowager Queen, and this was her twelfth pregnancy. On 18 July 1548, Edward VI's page, John Fowler, wrote to Thomas Seymour about the outcome of the duchess's delivery: "My Lady of Somerset is brought to bed of a goodly boy,

"A second court"

thanks be it to God; and, I trust in almighty God, the Queen's Grace shall have another".[18]

Katherine Parr, although sickly and much weakened, enjoyed her pregnancy. In her correspondence with Thomas Seymour, she affectionately called the baby "little knave" and hoped it would be a boy: "I gave your little knave your blessing, who like an honest man stirred apace after and before, for Mary Odell, being abed with me, had laid her hand upon my belly to feel it stir."[19] Mary Odell was Katherine Parr's beloved lady-in-waiting and a distant cousin on her mother's side. They were clearly on intimate terms, Mary being Katherine's customary bedfellow.

On 30 August 1548, Katherine Parr gave birth to her long-awaited child. The "little knave" turned out to be a girl, who was named Mary, after Henry VIII's elder daughter. The baby's sex did not matter to Katherine and Thomas, who took a great delight in their infant child. Thomas immediately penned a letter to his brother Edward, praising his daughter's beauty. The Lord Protector wrote back, addressing his letter to "my very good sister and brother". The letter is couched in the most affectionate terms, but it is underpinned by brotherly rivalry. Although Edward congratulated Thomas on the birth of "so pretty a daughter", he expressed regret that "this, the first" was not a son. Yet the fact that the Dowager Queen had successfully given birth and had a "happy hour", a good delivery, made Edward happy.[20] Yet within days Katherine Parr's health deteriorated, and it soon became apparent that she would succumb to the much-dreaded childbed fever.

As Katherine lay dying in her darkened bedchamber in the lavishly decorated Sudeley Castle, Elizabeth Tyrwhitt, one of the Dowager Queen's closest ladies-in-waiting, was taking care of her. Lady Tyrwhitt started her career as Jane Seymour's maid of honour in 1537 and served all of the subsequent wives of Henry VIII. Like Katherine, Lady Tyrwhitt enjoyed religious discussions and followed into Katherine Parr's footsteps in 1574 when she published her *Morning and Evening Prayers*. Just hours before Katherine Parr died, she complained to Elizabeth about Thomas Seymour's errant behaviour: "My lady Tyrwhitt, I am not well handled, for those that be about me careth not for me, but standeth laughing at my grief." Thomas's reaction proves that he thought Katherine was pointing an accusatory finger at him: "Why, sweetheart, I would do you no hurt." Still sharp of mind despite impending death, Katherine shook her head and complained that Seymour gave her "many shrewd taunts" over the course of their marriage, referring, perhaps, to his relationship with her stepdaughter Elizabeth. Thomas crawled into Katherine's bed, trying desperately to "pacify her unquietness with gentle communication".[21] She died of puerperal fever on 5 September 1548.

"A second court"

Within seven months of Katherine's death, Thomas Seymour's feud with his brother turned deadly. Thomas's deluded ambitions and Edward's drive for vengeance brought Thomas to the scaffold, where he lost his life on 20 March 1549. His infant daughter, Mary, was now effectively an orphan. Edward Seymour took her into his household during Thomas's imprisonment and arranged for an allowance to be paid to her from the royal treasury, but it was never Thomas Seymour's wish to see his only child raised by a brother who sent him to his death. He naively believed that since his late wife and Katherine Brandon, Duchess of Suffolk, were great friends, the duchess would prove to be an excellent guardian for the infant Mary Seymour.

This was a miscalculation on Thomas's part because the duchess regarded Mary Seymour as an expensive burden. As a daughter of a queen, the seven-month-old infant came to the duchess's household with a large retinue of servants. The duchess maintained that she had no money to support this semi-regal establishment and complained that Edward Seymour and his imperious wife failed to provide the promised allowance for their niece. Anne Seymour promised Katherine Brandon that Mary's valuable possessions would be sent with her, but in reality the Duchess of Somerset appropriated them for her own use. Katherine Brandon wrote to the duchess "that there may be some pension allotted" to

Great Ladies

Mary Seymour, yet no answer was forthcoming.[22] Furious that she had no financial help in supporting Mary Seymour's household, Katherine Brandon wrote to the Lord Protector's chief secretary, William Cecil. She complained that with such a financial burden, she would be unable to pay off her debts. The letter reveals that Mary Seymour's closest relatives shirked from their responsibilities towards her.

Katherine Parr's brother William "hath as weak a back for such a burden as I have", the Duchess of Suffolk wrote.[23] Mary Seymour was eventually restored to her executed father's lands and titles, and in March 1550 the Privy Council granted her money for wages, food and her servants' uniforms. This was the last mention of Katherine Parr's daughter in contemporary sources. An epitaph written by the Dowager Queen's chaplain reveals that Mary died in her early childhood. The epitaph says that she had a "brief life", and the fact that provision for her household was not renewed either in 1550 or in 1551 proves beyond doubt that she died around that time.[24]

NOTES

[1] Janel Mueller, *Katherine Parr: Complete Works and Correspondence,* p. 135.
[2] Ibid.
[3] Ibid., p. 186.
[4] *The Chronicle of King Henry VIII,* p. 161.

"A second court"

[5] In her book, _Katherine the Queen: The Remarkable Life of Katherine Parr_ (p. 298), historian Linda Porter stated that "there is no contemporary corroboration of such a quarrel", which is not correct.

[6] Susan James, _Catherine Parr: Henry VIII's Last Love_, p. 290.

[7] Ibid., p. 273.

[8] Janel Mueller, _Katherine Parr: Complete Works and Correspondence_, p. 141.

[9] Susan James, _Catherine Parr: Henry VIII's Last Love_, p. 277.

[10] Ibid.

[11] _A Collection of State Papers_, 1542-1570, p. 99.

[12] Ibid.

[13] Sarah Gristwood, _Arbella: England's Lost Queen_, p. 335.

[14] _A Collection of State Papers,_ op.cit.

[15] Ibid.

[16] Janel Mueller, _Katherine Parr: Complete Works and Correspondence_, p. 192.

[17] Ibid.

[18] Ibid., p. 173.

[19] Ibid., p. 170.

[20] Ibid., p. 175.

[21] Ibid., p. 177.

[22] Ibid., p. 185.

[23] Ibid., p. 187.

[24] Linda Porter, "Lady Mary Seymour: An Unfit Traveller", _History Today_, Volume 61 Issue 7.

CHAPTER 13
"SHE WENT OUT WEEPING"

Edward Seymour's reputation never recovered after his brother's execution, but it was his wife who was blamed for the Lord Protector's unpopular actions. Many believed that it was Anne Seymour, Duchess of Somerset, who convinced her husband that he must send his brother to the block to feel safe. This view stemmed from Anne's close relationship with her husband; it was a widely held belief that Anne's sway over Edward was malicious, but women were often blamed for their husbands' misdeeds in sixteenth-century England.[1] In the absence of a Queen consort at Edward VI's side, Anne Seymour became the most influential woman at court, and petitioners often appealed to her for help.

Henry VIII's elder daughter, Lady Mary, forged a long-lasting friendship with her that overcame religious differences between them. It seems improbable that Lady Mary, known for her staunchly Catholic views, befriended the woman who, by 1547, had established herself as a patroness of evangelical writers. But Lady Mary always felt fierce loyalty towards her late mother's servants, and it is clear that her relationship

"She went out weeping"

with the Duchess of Somerset hearkened back to the times when Anne Seymour, then known as Mistress Stanhope, served as Katharine of Aragon's maid of honour. In one of Mary's letters to her "good gossip", as she affectionately referred to Anne, she requested Anne speak with her husband about "mine old suit concerning Richard Wood, who was my mother's servant when you were one of her Grace's maids".[2] The Duchess of Somerset was fond of Lady Mary, as evidenced by Mary's effusive note wherein she thanked Anne "with all my heart for your earnest gentleness towards me in all my suits hitherto, reckoning myself out of doubt of the continuance of the same".[3] It is clear that Anne wanted to cultivate Mary's good graces and that she interceded with her husband on her behalf. Mary's suit was granted, and she later thanked Edward Seymour "for his attention to her requests as to pensions for some of her servants".[4]

By 1549, Edward Seymour's popularity as Lord Protector had dramatically decreased. The factors that contributed to his downfall were the ongoing war with Scotland that depleted the royal treasury and multiple rebellions stemming out of hostility towards Seymour's economic and religious policies. He also alienated many men and women at court when he refused to follow his fellow councillors' advices and adopted a regal "we" in his letters. Seymour's arrest on 11 October 1549 took him by surprise.

Edward VI, who kept a diary, recorded that his uncle was arrested because of his "ambition, vainglory, entering into rash wars in mine youth, negligent looking on Newhaven, enriching himself of my treasure, following his own opinion, and doing all by his own authority, etc."[5]

Some believed that bad decisions on Seymour's part were because he had "allowed himself to be ruled by his wife" and when he sent Anne away from court shortly before his arrest, "she went out weeping, very badly handled in words by the courtiers and peasants, who put all this trouble down to her".[6] As soon as she reached her home, Anne sat down to compose a letter to William Paget, a man of "great wisdom and friendly nature". She exhorted him to help her husband and clear him from slander. "I know you may do much good in these matters being a wise man", she wrote. The duchess believed that her husband was framed because she knew he was innocent of the charges laid against him. These charges were so "untrue and most unfriendly" that she believed that "some wicked person or persons" sought her beloved husband's destruction.[7] Fearing that Edward Seymour faced imminent execution, his devoted wife engaged herself in a campaign to release him from the Tower of London. On Christmas Day 1549, she "came unto him to the Tower to his no little comfort".[8] Furthermore, she decided to ally herself with her husband's political opponent.

"She went out weeping"

The man who engineered Somerset's arrest was John Dudley, Earl of Warwick, the Duke's erstwhile political partner and supporter. He was the son of Henry VII's financial minister Edmund Dudley, who had been executed during the early reign of Henry VIII. His father's execution was not an impediment to Dudley's career; he was knighted in 1523 and by 1533 he was made Master of the Armoury in the Tower of London. He served as Master of the Horse in Anne of Cleves's household in 1540 and three years later was created Viscount Lisle. In 1543, he became Lord Admiral and later that year joined the Privy Council and was elected as a member of the Order of the Garter. Henry VIII was fond of John Dudley and made him an executor to his last will in 1547, leaving him a substantial legacy of £500.

Anne Seymour was quick to notice Dudley's growing influence in 1549 and decided to explore her friendship with his wife to her best advantage. In December, it was said that Anne was "always in his [Dudley's] house" and won him over to her husband's cause.[9] By February 1550, Edward Seymour was released from the Tower. He had lost his post of Lord Protector—the title was abolished altogether as Dudley preferred the less controversial post of Lord President of the Privy Council—but he was allowed to retain his dukedom and place on the council. On 3 June 1550, the Dudley-Seymour alliance was strengthened when Edward Seymour's eldest daughter, named Anne after her mother, married John Dudley's eldest son, named John after him. "It is said that the two mothers have made the match", observed the new imperial ambassador, Jehan Scheyvfe.[10]

Jane Dudley, Countess of Warwick, was the daughter of Edward Guildford and his first wife, Eleanor West, daughter of Thomas West, Lord de la Warr. She served five of Henry VIII's six wives and became an influential member of Katherine Parr's Privy Chamber. Jane understood Anne Seymour's predicament, and it was she who convinced her husband that the Duke of Somerset should be released from the Tower. Yet the two women were unable to mend the relations between their husbands. Tensions between Dudley and Seymour intensified in 1551, when the imperial ambassador reported that "the Duke and my Lord of Warwick fell into a dispute in open Council, but the matter was soon calmed down".[11] Seymour resented Dudley's growing influence and felt that he was better qualified to govern, not only because of his merits but also because he was Edward VI's uncle.

In October 1551, Dudley was created Duke of Northumberland and arrested Seymour once again when he learned about Seymour's plot to overthrow him. Anne Seymour shared her husband's opinions and actively participated in the conspiracy. John Dudley was well aware of Anne's political influence and sent her to the Tower as well.

"She went out weeping"

"As she is guarded there with great care, we are ignorant as to what offence she is suffering", wrote Thomas Norton, Edward Seymour's secretary, to John Calvin in November 1551.[12] Some even believed that "she was not imprisoned for having committed a crime, but to prevent her from committing one".[13]

As the King's relatives, Edward and Anne Seymour were lodged in comfortable confinement in the Tower of London. Each had servants to tend to their daily needs; the duke had four attendants, the duchess three.[14] Both had also requested fine clothing and plate to be brought from their luxurious manor house. The duke "prayed to have" such things like a velvet cap, night cap, two pairs of velvet shoes, two doublets, three shirts, tablecloths, napkins and towels. The duchess ordered twice as many items of clothing; she may have been a prisoner, but she was determined to look every inch a high-status noblewoman. She ordered such items as a velvet waistcoat, two pairs of knitted hose, one pair of woollen hose, seven newly made "plain smocks", seven high-collared partlets with detachable ruffs, a gown of black velvet edged with genets, two pairs of gloves and leather slippers from her private wardrobe.[15] It is also clear that the duchess wanted to pass her time in reading and sewing. She had three "little books covered with black velvet" delivered to her and also "some black silk and white thread".[16]

Great Ladies

Despite all these comforts, Edward Seymour was executed on 22 January 1552. Anne firmly believed that she would follow Edward to the scaffold. Only days after her husband's death, she requested the Bishop of Gloucester visit her "for the settling of her conscience".[17] On 12 February 1552, the imperial ambassador noted that people widely believed that she "will soon go the same way".[18] Yet this was not to happen. The duchess's life was never endangered, but she remained imprisoned until the end of Edward VI's reign.

NOTES

[1] Anne Boleyn, for example, was blamed for Henry VIII's decision to execute Sir Thomas More in 1535.

[2] Patrick Fraser Tytler, *England Under the Reigns of Edward VI and Mary*, Volume 1, p. 51.

[3] Ibid.

[4] *Calendar of State Papers, Domestic Series, of the Reigns of Edward VI, Mary, Elizabeth, 1547-1580*, p. 5.

[5] Jonathan North, *England's Boy King: The Diary of Edward VI, 1547-1553*, p. 22.

[6] *Calendar of State Papers, Spain*, Volume 9, 1547-1549, entries for 13 August and 8 October 1549.

[7] *The Letters of William, Lord Paget of Beaudesert, 1547-63*, p. 33.

[8] *Letters of Richard Scudamore to Sir Philip Hoby*, Volume 39 of Camden Fourth Series, p. 104.

[9] *Calendar of State Papers, Spain*, Volume 9, 1547-1549, entry for 19 December 1549.

[10] *Calendar of State Papers, Spain*, Volume 10, 1550-1552, entry for 6 June 1550.

[11] Ibid., 9 April 1551.

[12] Hastings Robinson, *Original Letters Relative to the English Reformation*, Volume 1, p. 342.

[13] Ibid.

[14] *Acts of the Privy Council of England*, Volume 3, p. 391.

"She went out weeping"

[15] Henry Ellis, *Original Letters, Illustrative of English History*, Volume 2, p. 215.

[16] Ibid.

[17] *Acts of the Privy Council of England*, Volume 3, p. 466.

[18] *Calendar of State Papers, Spain,* Volume 10, 1550-1552, entry for 12 February 1552.

CHAPTER 14
"A FLOCK OF PEERESSES"

With Anne Seymour imprisoned, it was Jane Dudley, now Duchess of Northumberland, who emerged as the most influential woman at court. In the absence of a Queen consort at Edward VI's side, Jane had an important role to fulfil: she was now the "primary hostess" at court.[1] All looked well for the Dudleys until the young King fell sick. In the spring of 1552, he simultaneously contracted measles and smallpox and survived only to succumb to tuberculosis. On 28 May 1553, the imperial ambassador described Edward VI's disease in vivid detail; the young King was in great pain and racked by fits of violent cough, his feet and body were swollen and "the sputum which he brings up is livid, black, fetid and full of carbon" and smelled "beyond measure".[2] It soon became apparent that Edward VI was dying.

The King's mind turned to succession. Despite his youth, Edward was zealously dedicated to religious reform. According to the terms of his father's 1544 Act of Succession, confirmed by Henry VIII's last will of 1547, Edward's elder half sister Mary stood to inherit the crown. Everyone in England knew that, and many assumed that Mary would soon become Queen. Edward was horrified by the prospect of Mary inheriting his kingdom because he knew she would bring Catholicism back and undo all his reforms. "I am convinced that my sister Mary would provoke great disturbances after I have left this life", he told his councillors, adding that he planned to disinherit both Mary and Elizabeth.[3] Edward reasoned that he had solid grounds to do so. After all, both of his half sisters had been declared Henry VIII's bastards and as illegitimate royal daughters could not inherit anything, much less the crown. Following the precedent set in his father's last will, Edward VI also bypassed the heirs of Henry VIII's elder sister, Margaret Tudor, Queen of Scots. This left the heirs of Edward's junior aunt, Mary Tudor, Dowager Queen of France, and her husband, Charles Brandon, Duke of Suffolk.

The exclusion of his elder half sister, Mary, seemed rational—Edward always tried to convert her, and he was not personally attached to her. The exclusion of Elizabeth seemed suspicious to most people who knew how close the young King was to his "Sweet Sister Temperance", as he affectionately referred to her. The two often exchanged correspondence, and at some point the King ordered Elizabeth's portrait. She was a frequent guest at his court and basked in his attention. Furthermore, she was of the same religious conviction as Edward. With both of his sisters out of the way, the King decided to leave his kingdom to the male offspring of his first cousin, Frances Grey. If she would have no sons, then the crown was to pass to the sons of Jane, Katherine or Mary Grey, Frances's daughters.

The Greys had close ties to the royal family. Frances Grey, née Brandon, was the daughter of Mary Tudor, Henry VIII's younger sister, and Charles Brandon, Duke of Suffolk. In 1533, she married Henry Grey, Marquess of Dorset, the great-grandson of Elizabeth Woodville and her first husband, John Grey of Groby. In 1551, Henry Grey was created Duke of Suffolk after the male line of the Brandon Dukes of Suffolk became extinct.

Frances and Henry had three daughters: Jane, Katherine and Mary. Jane Grey, the eldest, was their pride and joy. She was raised in the teachings of the New Religion and was more pious than her young age merited. She was also exceptionally talented and preferred reading Greek philosophers to hunting, as her tutor Roger Ascham later recorded in his memoirs. Ascham believed that Jane was naturally inclined to read great classical philosophers because she derived her birth "both on your father's side and on your mother's from kings and queens".[4]

In the spring of 1553, Edward VI drew up his "devise for the succession". "For the lack of issue male of my body", the frail King bequeathed his kingdom "to the issue male coming of the issue female, as I have after declared. To the

"A flock of peeresses"

Lady Frances's heirs males, if she have any; for lack of such issue before my death, to the Lady Jane's heirs males; to the Lady Katherine's heirs males; to the Lady Mary's heirs males; to the heirs males of the daughters which she [Frances Grey] shall have hereafter. . ."[5] The devise also specified that if these women failed to produce male heirs, the crown was to pass on to the male offspring of Margaret Clifford, Frances's niece.[6] The early draft of the King's devise makes it clear that he did not originally plan to be succeeded by a female. It was only after he realised that he would die sooner than any male heir was born to his kinswomen that he decided for a radical change of the document. "If I die without issue and there be none heir male", Edward reiterated once again, "then the Lady Frances to be Governess Regent . . . until some heir male be born, and then the mother of that child to be Governess". The situation envisaged by the dying King was politically dangerous and he soon changed his devise for the last time. He was now convinced that Lady Jane Grey was eminently suitable to become his successor since she was of royal descent and Protestant faith. The phrase "Lady Jane's heirs males" was altered to "Lady Jane *and her* heirs male".[7] With the addition of just two short words, Jane Grey became heiress to the throne.

Edward VI died on 6 July 1553, but his death was kept in strict secrecy. Jane was at Chelsea manor, the former residence of Katherine Parr, when she was informed that she had to be conveyed to Syon House. There, the leading members of nobility acknowledged her as their new sovereign lady, to Jane's "extreme confusion". She was apparently so distraught that the Duke of Northumberland had to wait with further announcements until the arrival of Frances Grey, Jane Dudley and Elisabeth Parr. Northumberland then informed Jane officially that Edward VI had died and made her his heiress. "Hearing these words, all the lords of the council kneeled before me", Jane later recalled. When the lords told her that the late King urged them "to shed their own blood freely, and to offer their own lives to death in this cause", she listened with "extreme grief of mind". Then, overcome "by sudden and unlooked for sorrow", the girl "fell to the ground, weeping very bitterly". She was inadequate, she said, and it grieved her to hear of the King's death. She accepted the dubious honor of becoming the first English Queen regnant with reluctance. "For although I took upon me that of which I was unworthy, yet no one can say that I ever sought to obtain it for myself, nor ever solaced myself therein, nor accepted it willingly", she recalled.[8]

Some chose to believe that John Dudley, Duke of Northumberland, stood behind Edward VI's decision since his son Guildford married Lady Jane on 25 May 1553. Jane's uncle said that "it seemed strange to him that the Lady Jane, and not

"A flock of peeresses"

her mother, had been chosen [as Edward VI's heiress], and that the Duke of Northumberland thus showed that the object of his ambition was to place the crown on the head of his son, husband to the Lady Jane".[9] But when Jane was presented with the royal jewels, she made it clear that her husband would not be crowned with her and that she would make him a duke rather than king. "This my resolution caused his mother, when it was reported to her, to find occasion for much wrath and disdain", Jane later remembered. Jane Dudley, Duchess of Northumberland, was "very angry" with Jane and "so displeased that she persuaded her son not to sleep with me any longer". The young woman clearly perceived her mother-in-law as imperious and overbearing. In retrospect, Jane Grey could say with a great deal of confidence that she was "deceived by the Duke and the council, and ill-treated by my husband and his mother".[10] She even firmly believed that poison was administered to her twice, once in the house of the Duke of Northumberland and then again in the Tower because the skin was peeling off her body.[11]

To John Dudley's astonishment, Mary Tudor claimed the throne without bloodshed. She perceived Jane Grey as Dudley's puppet and made it clear from the start of her reign that she intended no harm to her young cousin. But she was not as merciful when it came to John Dudley and Henry Grey,

Great Ladies

who were arrested. Dudley's sons, including Guildford, were also placed in the Tower.

It was now left to the women to defend their families' reputations and plead with Queen Mary. On 2 August 1553, Frances Grey arrived at Beaulieu Palace, the Queen's residence, to beg her to release her husband. Frances informed the Queen that John Dudley had attempted to poison Henry Grey—rumors that Dudley poisoned Edward VI made the rounds at court, and even Lady Jane claimed that she was envenomed in Dudley's residence, so Frances hoped that the accusation would stick.[12] Frances Grey is often accused of being a callous mother who did not try to save her daughter's life, but it was well known at court that the Queen intended to begin her reign mercifully and spare Jane's life. Although Mary planned to put Jane Grey on trial for treason, she said that her conscience "would not permit her to have her put to death".[13] Henry Grey, Jane's father, was released on 31 July 1553.[14]

The Duke of Northumberland's wife also tried to plead with Queen Mary. Jane Dudley was imprisoned in the Tower for about a week after Mary was proclaimed Queen on 19 July 1553, and she and her sons reportedly received "sour treatment".[15] On 29 July 1553, the imperial ambassador reported:

"A flock of peeresses"

"The Duchess of Northumberland has been let out of prison sooner than was expected, and set out to meet the Queen to move her to compassion towards her children; but when she had arrived at a spot five miles from this place, the Queen ordered her to return to London, and refused to give her audience."[16]

The last thing Queen Mary wanted was to see Jane Dudley interceding with her on behalf of her husband and sons. Mary blamed John Dudley for trying to steal away her royal inheritance, and she was bent on executing him. But the Duchess of Northumberland was not about to give up. She knew that Mary was inclined to show mercy and hoped that she would forgive her husband. To achieve her goal, the duchess wrote a letter to Anne Paget, wife of the influential courtier William Paget. Paget made a brilliant career under Henry VIII and Edward VI and transferred his allegiance to Queen Mary. He was instrumental in the reconciliation of a number of his colleagues to the Queen after what Mary perceived was Northumberland's coup to put Jane Grey on the throne. Lady Paget immediately became the Queen's lady-in-waiting and had access not only to the Queen herself but, above all, to her favorites.

In the summer of 1553, one woman especially stood in Mary's affection: Gertrude Courtenay, Marchioness of Exeter. Queen Mary was fiercely loyal to her old friends and was now in a position to reward them. Gertrude, who had lingered in obscurity since her husband's execution in 1538, was one of the Queen's favorites. Mary never forgot that Gertrude was her mother's loyal friend and supporter and summoned her to court as soon as she knew she won against Dudley. Gertrude was among 180 ladies and gentlemen who entered the City of London in the Queen's entourage on 3 August 1553.

Mary's entry was a riot of color: she rode on her richly caparisoned horse dressed in a French gown of purple velvet with matching sleeves embroidered with gold and a kirtle thickly set with pearls. Rich golden necklaces and chains glistened around her neck, and her French hood was adorned with shiny pearls and stones. Behind her rode Sir Anthony Browne, Master of the Horse, "leaning on her horse, having the train of her Highness's gown hanging over his shoulder".[17] Following him were the most prominent women of Mary's newly formed household: the Queen's twenty-year-old half sister, Elizabeth, now effectively heiress to the throne, followed by Gertrude Courtenay and Elizabeth Howard, Duchess of Norfolk. A "flock of peeresses, gentlewomen and ladies-in-waiting, never before seen in such numbers", followed after them.[18]

That day was not only a great triumph for Mary, but also a moment of joy and elation for Gertrude Courtenay. When the royal cavalcade entered the Tower of London, she caught a glimpse of a young man with a forked beard and dark eyes. Kneeling by the Tower Gate was her only son, Edward, imprisoned since 1538. He was not alone: Thomas Howard, Duke of Norfolk; Stephen Gardiner, Bishop of Winchester; and Anne Seymour, Duchess of Somerset, were all there, prisoners of the regimes of Henry VIII and Edward VI, all pleading for pardon.[19] The scene was staged to show how merciful Mary Tudor intended to be. She approached them, kissed them and granted them their long-awaited freedom.[20]

In August 1553, Gertrude Courtenay's influence with the Queen was so high that she immediately became Mary's bedfellow, sleeping with the Queen in her bedchamber and sharing her most guarded secrets. The other woman who was very close to Mary was Susan Clarencius, who had loyally served her since the 1530s and was one of her closest friends and confidantes. Jane Dudley knew that these women could help her sway the Queen. Her letter to Anne Paget is not only a testament to her perseverance and love for her family, but also a proof that she knew who to flatter:

"Now good Madam, for the love you bear to God, forget me not and make my Lady Marchioness of Exeter my good lady to remember me to Mistress Clarencius, to continue as she had before for me. Good Madam, desire your lord as he may do in speaking for my husband's life: In a way of charity I crave him to do it."[21]

She went on to say that her family's troubles aggravated her health problems and she began to "grow into weakness". The postscript she added to the letter is especially touching because it reveals the strength of her love for her husband: "Good Madam, desire my lord to be good lord unto my poor five sons: nature can no otherwise do but sue for them, although I do not so much care for them as for their father who was to me and to my mind the best gentleman that ever a living woman was matched withal . . ."[22]

Yet her pleas for John Dudley's release were unsuccessful. On 18 August 1553, he was tried and sentenced to death. To the astonishment of those who knew him, Dudley converted to Catholicism, perhaps in the hope of Queen Mary sparing him. She did not. Dudley was executed on 22 August 1553.

Whether Gertrude Courtenay and Susan Clarencius pleaded for his life remains uncertain but likely. The imperial ambassadors reported that they did intercede, with much success, on behalf of William Parr, Marquess of Northampton, who was involved in Dudley's plot. Jane Dudley's last will provides some clue as to who might have been interceding on her family's behalf with the Queen. To Susan Clarencius, she left "my tawny velvet jewel-coffer", to Lady Anne Paget "my high-backed gown of wrought velvet", to William Paget "one of my black enameled rings I did use to wear" and to Lady

"A flock of peeresses"

Margaret Sandys another ring not as valuable as the one given to Paget.[23] Notably, Gertrude Courtenay received nothing from Jane Dudley, and this may well indicate that she was not involved in helping her.

Before her husband's downfall, Jane Dudley was a wealthy Tudor matron in the making. The register of clothes and precious materials such as cloth of gold, wrought black velvet, crimson velvet and many others, confiscated by Queen Mary shortly after John's arrest, reveal the great wealth the Dudleys had amassed over the years.24 After John Dudley's fall, his wife was "stripped almost of all necessities of life" and had to rely on the Queen's charity.25 On 4 September 1553, the imperial ambassadors reported that they heard rumors that Jane's sons were to be spared, and the duchess herself received "an income of 4,000 crowns, a furnished house and a pension of 300 crowns, besides (the enjoyment of) her own private possessions".26 But the duchess did not know if her sons were to be released and continued lobbying the influential members of Queen Mary's court until the end of her life.

NOTES

[1] Catherine Medici, *"More than a Wife and Mother: Jane Dudley, the Woman Who Bequeathed a Parrot And Served Five Queens"*, p. 260.
[2] Elizabeth Lane Furdell, *The Royal Doctors, 1485-1714*, p. 50.
[3] Anna Whitelock, *Mary Tudor: England's First Queen*, p. 139.

Great Ladies

[4] Roger Ascham, *The Whole Works of Roger Ascham*, Volume I, p. 239.

[5] *The Honourable Society of the Inner Temple*: Edward VI's "My devise for the succession", Inner Temple Library, Petyt MS 538.47, f. 317.

[6] She was a daughter of Eleanor Clifford, née Brandon, Duchess of Cumberland, who died in 1547.

[7] Edward VI's "My devise for the succession", op.cit.

[8] *Writings of Edward VI*, p. 29.

[9] *Calendar of State Papers, Spain,* Volume 11, 1553, entry for 24 July 1553.

[10] *Writings of Edward VI*, pp. 30-32.

[11] Ibid.

[12] *Calendar of State Papers, Spain,* Volume 11, 1553, entry for 2 August 1553.

[13] Ibid., entry for 16 August 1553.

[14] Charles Wriothesley, *Wriothesley's Chronicle*, Volume 2, p. 92.

[15] Ibid., entry for 22 July 1553.

[16] Ibid., entry for 29 July 1553.

[17] Charles Wriothesley, *Wriothesley's Chronicle*, Volume 2, p. 93.

[18] Ibid.

[19] John Gough Nichols, *The Chronicle of Queen Jane and of Two Years of Queen Mary*, p. 14.

[20] Ibid.

[21] S. J. Gunn, "A Letter of Jane, Duchess of Northumberland, in 1553", *English Historical Review*, November 1999.

[22] Ibid.

[23] TNA PROB 11/37/342: The last will of Jane Dudley, Duchess of Northumberland.

[24] Arthur Collins, *Letters and Memorials of State*, p. 33.

[25] Ibid.

[26] *Calendar of State Papers, Spain,* Volume 11, 1553, entry for 4 September 1553.

CHAPTER 15
"THE QUEEN'S MOST INTIMATE CONFIDANTES"

Mary Tudor was England's first Queen regnant. Not since Empress Matilda claimed the throne in 1141 had the country seen a woman rule in her own right. Matilda, being King Henry I's legitimate daughter, had a strong claim to the throne, but England was not ready for a female monarch, and Matilda's claim was challenged by her cousin, Stephen of Blois. With Mary, it was different because she ascended the throne on a wave of popular rejoicing. She was an immensely popular figure, and people had widely empathised with her during her father's divorce from Katharine of Aragon. Edward VI might have been a brilliant ruler if he had gotten a chance to grow into maturity, but England was literally governed by the men about Edward, and so the country did not have a strong monarchical presence. Mary, despite her sex, was a Tudor and the true heiress of her father.

The accession of England's first Queen regnant necessitated changes in the structure of the royal household. Royal courts were predominantly male preserves, with women playing minor roles. Some governed their husbands behind the scenes, but they never had real power or influence over politics. Mary's accession changed this. Men still filled important positions in the government, but they were now effectively excluded from the Queen's Privy Chamber. As a woman, Mary surrounded herself with female companions who filled important posts around her. The Queen never fully developed self-confidence, and she felt she needed guidance.

These women, who knew Mary well, understood that they could obtain various favours for themselves and their relatives because of the Queen's inability to refuse them. In August 1553, Charles V's ambassadors complained that "the ladies about the Queen's person are able to obtain from her more than she ought to grant them".[1] They would soon try to influence the most important decision of Mary's reign.

At thirty-seven, Mary was deemed too old to marry or beget children, but she made it clear that she intended to take a spouse for the sake of England's well-being. In the privacy of the Queen's apartments, "the ladies who surrounded her talked of nothing else but marriage", trying to feel their royal mistress's mood.[2] The Queen's marriage was a matter of deep concern for Mary's councillors and subjects alike. Women were expected to show complete subservience to their husbands, and many feared that if Mary married a foreigner, he would govern the nation in her stead. These fears were justified. As far back as in 1518, when Mary was engaged to

"The Queen's most intimate confidantes"

the French dauphin, a Venetian diplomat observed that "the sole fear of this kingdom" was "that it may pass into the power of the French through this marriage".[3]

The English were bent on convincing the Queen to marry one of her subjects. Their hopes focused on Edward Courtenay, son of Mary's favourite lady-in-waiting, Gertrude Courtenay, Marchioness of Exeter. In his mid-twenties, Courtenay was young, handsome and of royal blood. His wits were not dulled by the fifteen years he had spent in the Tower. The imperial ambassadors reported that he received excellent education and thus "his incarceration, his prison and confinement have not been grievous to him, but have been converted into liberty by his studiousness and taste for letters and science". Despite growing up away from court, the ambassadors judged that there was "civility" in Courtenay, which they thought "must be deemed natural rather than acquired by the habit of society; and his bodily graces are in proportion to those of his mind".[4] Mary felt personally responsible for his well-being and heaped favour after favour upon him, creating him Earl of Devon and Knight of the Bath. But despite "much talk here to the effect that he will be married to the Queen as he is of the blood royal", Mary had no intention of marrying Courtenay.[5]

Yet Courtenay was dazzled by the attention he received from people as he was "courted and followed about by the whole Court". Many sought employment in his household and started treating him as a king-in-waiting. Courtenay soon grew so confident that he started calling Stephen Gardiner, Bishop of Winchester, "his father, and Dame Clarencius his mother".[6] This anecdote shows that Susan Clarencius was the most trusted and closest female servant of the Queen. Indeed, she was one of only three ladies-in-waiting whose trust Mary never doubted.

Mary maintained that she had "no liking for Courtenay", yet his mother Gertrude still supported his candidacy for the Queen's hand.[7] It was Gertrude's fervent wish to see herself and her son rewarded for the years of adversity they suffered at Henry VIII's hands. Gertrude supported Mary during the turbulent 1530s, and her husband was executed amid rumours that the White Rose party intended to oust Henry VIII and replace him with his daughter. Yet Mary had no intention of marrying her subject and soon conceived a strong dislike for Courtenay. This reflected on her relationship with Gertrude, who lost her position as Mary's favourite.

Mary quickly learned that she had to bestow her favors carefully. One woman who was Mary's closest friend and confidante, and who appeared to have no agenda of her own was Susan Clarencius. The exact date of her birth remains unknown, but she seems to have been something of a mother figure to the Queen, who loved and cherished Susan more than any other woman at court. According to a reliable contemporary source, Susan served in Mary's household since Mary's childhood and was "respected and beloved by the Queen".[8] By 1553, Susan was widowed, childless and much devoted to her royal mistress. She was Mary's Lady Almoness, Mistress of the Robes and chief Lady of the Bedchamber. Susan knew Mary's true feelings about marriage. If the Queen were a private individual, she would never have desired marriage since "she preferred to end her days in chastity".[9] But as a monarch, she owed it to her subjects to beget a child who would succeed her.

On a more personal level, Mary saw her marriage as the means of ousting her despised half sister from the line of succession. The Queen was heard saying that she would not allow Elizabeth to be her heiress "because of her heretical opinions, illegitimacy and characteristics in which she resembled her mother".[10] Seventeen years after Anne Boleyn's execution, Mary was still haunted by the memory of a woman whom she blamed for her own mother's misfortunes.

On 10 October 1553, Simon Renard, the imperial ambassador whom Mary liked and trusted, had offered her the hand in marriage of Prince Philip of Spain. Philip was Charles V's son, and Mary had always treated the Holy Roman Emperor as a father figure. Fiercely proud of her Spanish roots, the Queen dreamed of reviving the Anglo-Spanish alliance and breeding a new line of Catholic princes and princesses with Tudor and Hapsburg blood running in their veins. On 29 October, Mary admitted Renard to her presence to accept Prince Philip as her husband. It was not an easy decision—ever since the ambassador proposed this match, Mary had barely slept and "continually wept and prayed God to inspire her with an answer to the question of marriage". Pointing at the Holy Sacrament, which stood on the altar before them, Mary told Renard that "she had invoked it as her protector, guide and counselor, and still prayed with all her heart that it would come to her help". "There was no one else in the room except Mrs Clarentius and myself", Renard later reported. They followed the Queen when she knelt before the sacrament, singing the religious hymn "Veni Creator Spiritus".

Susan Clarentius was privy to the most important moment of Mary's life, but it was hardly surprising to Renard, who was by now used to her presence during his private audiences with the Queen. Yet Renard was sceptical about Susan's understanding of that solemn moment, perhaps because he spoke with Mary in Spanish, and Susan was not proficient in that language. "I do not know whether Clarentius knew the meaning of all this", he mused, "though I think she did because of the affection she showed me".[11] Several days later Renard reported that "Mrs Clarentius has made known

"The Queen's most intimate confidantes"

her decree, and supports our cause to the utmost".[12] The ambassador acknowledged Susan's efforts on behalf of the Spanish match, and in a letter to the Holy Roman Emperor Charles V, he produced an impressive list of those courtiers he thought Prince Philip should reward when he arrived in England. "Dame Clarencius" was included together with "another lady-in-waiting and two women who have been faithful and discreet and have always been present when I have negotiated with the Queen".[13] Their efforts were so important that Renard felt obliged to remind Charles V about Philip's gifts:

"And your Majesty understands that His Highness, on arriving here, will have to present a few rings and other trifles to the Queen's ladies and more substantial tokens to the three chief ones, named Clarentius, [Frideswide] Strelley and [Jane] Russell, who have always stood firm for the match and are the Queen's most intimate confidantes".[14]

These three women started their service within Mary's household long before she became Queen and now offered their emotional support. Mary needed encouragement. She wanted to marry, but she always maintained that she had never given much thought to love matters and desired only to fulfill her duties as a sovereign. As a woman, she was expected to marry and produce heirs. These seemingly private decisions became matters of state when Mary became Queen.

Great Ladies

Embarking upon childbearing at her age and after a history of menstrual irregularities was hazardous, and Mary certainly feared that by agreeing to marry Prince Philip she might have well signed her death warrant. But she always placed duty above her personal inclinations, although it is clear that Mary longed to create a family of her own.

NOTES

[1] *Calendar of State Papers, Spain,* Volume 11, entry for 27 August 1553.
[2] Ibid., entry for 8 September 1553.
[3] *Calendar of State Papers, Venice,* Volume 2, 1509-1519, n. 1103.
[4] *Calendar of State Papers, Spain,* Volume 11, entry for 22 July 1553.
[5] Ibid.
[6] Ibid., entry for 19 September 1553.
[7] Ibid., entry for 23 October 1553.
[8] Henry Clifford, *The Life of Jane Dormer, Duchess of Feria,* p. 132.
[9] *Calendar of State Papers, Spain,* Volume 11, entry for 2 August 1553.
[10] Ibid., entry for 28 November 1553.
[11] Ibid., entry for 31 October 1553.
[12] Ibid., entry for 6 November 1553.
[13] Ibid., entry for 28 November 1553.
[14] Ibid., entry for 8 March 1554.

CHAPTER 16
"HARBOUR OF HONOURABLE GENTLEWOMEN"

The announcement of the Queen's impending marriage to Prince Philip of Spain was greeted with discontent among her subjects. On 16 November 1553, some twenty members of the Commons appeared before Mary to dissuade her from marrying a foreigner, but she eloquently explained her own stance on the matter. She refused to be forced into marrying Edward Courtenay, declaring that "if she were married against her will she would not live three months and she would have no children".[1] Mary implied that if she married someone she did not like, she would be unable to conceive. The news of Mary's intended Spanish alliance spread through England like wildfire, and by the end of the year a conspiracy aiming at thwarting the Spanish match by deposing the Queen and replacing her with her half sister, Elizabeth, and Edward Courtenay was hatched. The leader of the rebellion was Sir Thomas Wyatt from Kent, son of the much-famed poet. The conspirators were backed by the French King Henri II, who hoped that the Anglo-Spanish alliance could be nipped in its bud.

The Queen was urged to seek refuge in the Tower of London or at Windsor, but she refused and stayed at Whitehall Palace with five hundred men ready to defend her. On 1 February 1554, she rode to Guildhall, where she delivered the most memorable speech of her reign. Addressing her "loving subjects" in her rough, manly voice, she declared that she was wedded to her realm and that although she had no children, she loved her people as mothers loved their offspring. She then explained that her decision to marry was not dictated by her whim but because "it might please God that I should leave you a successor". "On the word of a Queen", she ensured them that she would never allow the Spaniards to oppress them. With this speech Mary had again won the hearts of her people, who cried out, "God save Queen Mary and the Prince of Spain!"[2]

Mary's resolve was so strong that she wanted to fight on the field herself, but this was not allowed. She stayed with her women at Whitehall and once again refused to flee. Whereas the Queen proved that she had great courage, her ladies-in-waiting gave vent to their fears. When an armed detachment of gentlemen pensioners stationed themselves under the Queen's suite, "the ladies were very fearful". They were "lamenting, crying and wringing their hands".[3] Fearing

"Harbour of honourable gentlewomen"

defeat, the ladies wailed: "Alas, there is some great mischief towards; we shall all be destroyed this night!" While others bewailed: "What a sight is this, to see the Queen's chamber full of armed men; the like was never seen or heard of."[4] But Wyatt and his rebels were defeated, and life at court soon returned to its natural rhythm.

The only exception was that this time the Queen did not hesitate to punish those who offended her. Jane Grey's father, the Duke of Suffolk, who joined the rebellion, was arrested, and this time his wife made no attempt to plead for his life. Jane Grey and her husband, Guildford Dudley, who had languished in the Tower since July 1553, were executed on 12 February 1554. Jane's fool of a father followed her to the scaffold on 23 February. In the last letter she penned to him, Jane wrote that "although it hath pleased God to hasten my death by you, by whom my life should rather have been lengthened", she greeted the end of her "woeful days" with joy.[5] Yet at the scaffold, when she was blindfolded and could not find the wooden block she was supposed to lay her neck on, she panicked. "What shall I do? Where is it?" she cried out, terrified. A touched bystander gently guided her to the block, where she put her head and stretched out her arms. An axe fell on her neck: "And so she ended."[6]

The Queen's ire also turned to her half sister, Elizabeth, since the rebels aimed at proclaiming her Queen. On

Great Ladies

the day of Jane Grey's execution, Elizabeth—sick and terrified—was summoned to court. She hoped to speak with the Queen, but Mary refused to see her. The Queen knew that her half sister's name was on the rebels' lips the entire time, and she suspected that Elizabeth had been forewarned about their plans. The evidence was damning since Wyatt acknowledged that he had sent Elizabeth a letter, to which she replied verbally, sending her servant with a message that "she did thank him much for his goodwill and she would do as she should see cause".[7] The sole fact that Elizabeth entered into communication with a traitor was damning enough. Simon Renard, the imperial ambassador Mary trusted, urged the Queen to send Elizabeth to the scaffold, but Mary would never stoop so low as to execute her once-cherished younger sibling. Elizabeth was briefly imprisoned in the Tower but was later released and placed under house arrest in the dilapidating palace of Woodstock.

With all threats removed, Mary could now return to planning her wedding. Prince Philip reached England in the summer and married Mary on 25 July 1554. The Spaniards who arrived in Philip's entourage were impressed neither with the Queen nor with her ladies. "The Queen is well served, with a household full of officials, great lords and gentlemen, as well as many ladies, most of whom are so far from beautiful as to be downright ugly, though I know not why this should be

"Harbour of honourable gentlewomen"

so, for outside the palace I have seen plenty of beautiful women with lovely faces", one anonymous member of Philip's household wrote spitefully.[8] He proclaimed that the Queen was "not at all beautiful: small, and rather flabby than fat, she is of white complexion and fair, and has no eyebrows".[9] He somewhat derided her piety when he wrote that she was "a perfect saint and dresses badly". He also mocked the clothes worn by Mary's ladies, writing that they were "very badly cut". This description of Mary and her female entourage shaped the perception of the Queen for centuries to come, yet it is clear that it was coloured by hatred towards the xenophobic English.

Other sources described Mary as very fashion-forward. Giacomo Soranzo, Venetian diplomat, reported that Mary delighted "above all in arraying herself elegantly and magnificently", adding that she wore "much embroidery, and gowns and mantles of cloth of gold and cloth of silver, of great value, and changes them every day".[10] Mary also loved jewellery and adorned her hands, neck and gowns with valuable pieces. On 10 December 1554, she "came out adorned with her brocades and jewels", and her ladies-in-waiting "all had head-dresses enriched with gold, and many of them jewels and silk fringes".[11] Mary used clothes to enhance her royal magnificence and delighted the onlookers with the richness of materials and jewels she selected. The only reason

Great Ladies

the unfriendly Spaniard disparaged the Queen's style was that she preferred French rather than Spanish gowns, and the French were the Spaniards' ancient enemies. It was not until 1556 that the Queen adopted the Spanish style, trying to appeal to her husband's tastes.

"We Spaniards move among the English as if they were animals, trying not to notice them; and they do the same to us", wrote the anonymous Spanish gentleman, and Simon Renard observed that the anti-Spanish feelings ran high at court. "There is the obstacle of language", the ambassador wrote, "and then, as I have often explained in my letters, the English hate strangers and have never seen so many of them at once".[12] The discontented Spaniards were offended at the treatment of Philip:

"They refuse to crown our Prince, though he is their King, for they do not recognise him as such or as in any way their superior, but merely as one who has come to act as governor of the realm and get the Queen with child. When she has had children of him, they say, he may go home to Spain. Would to God it might happen at once! For it would be a good thing for him and I believe he would be very glad; we certainly should all be delighted to get away from these barbarous folk."[13]

"Harbour of honourable gentlewomen"

By an act of parliament, Mary was the "sole Queen", who ruled as absolutely as if she were King. Mary the Queen was separated from Mary, wife of Philip. To emphasize Philip's inferiority, she gave him the lodgings previously occupied by Queens consort and herself claimed the King's side of the royal household. These injunctions were aimed at curbing Philip's royal power—he was to be Mary's consort and nothing more.

Philip took it all patiently and tried to ingratiate himself with his new subjects. Mary had instantly fallen in love with this tall and handsome twenty-seven-year-old man, and he masked his true feelings by showing her much kindness and affection. Whereas it was easy for Mary to fall love with the charming Philip, he reckoned that she was "no good from the point of view of fleshly sensuality".[14] Mary was described as good-looking when younger, but a life marked by sorrow and health problems generated by menstrual irregularities aged her prematurely. "She is of spare and delicate frame", wrote the Venetian ambassador who saw her, adding that her face was "well formed". Her eyes were described as "white and large" and "so piercing that they inspire not only respect, but fear, in those on whom she fixes them". She was extremely shortsighted and had to look closely at people and documents. Her voice was "rough and loud, almost like a man's, so that when she speaks she is always heard a long way off". "In short", concluded the ambassador, "she is a seemly woman, and never to be loathed for ugliness, even at her present age".[15] One of the members of Philip's entourage, Ruy Gómez de Silva, empathised with his royal master when he wrote that "it would take God himself to drink this cup", referring to the consummation of the match, adding that "the best one can say is that the King realises fully that the marriage was made for no fleshly consideration, but in order to cure the disorders of this country and to preserve the Low Countries".[16]

In November 1554, Mary announced that she was expecting a child and that she felt it moving inside her womb. She was expected to give birth on 9 May 1555, and the necessary preparations were made in advance. The Queen experienced typical signs of pregnancy; her menstruation ceased, her belly was enlarged and her breasts emitted milk. She was so sure of her condition that in April 1555 she summoned her half sister, Elizabeth, to court so that she could be present when the heir who displaced her in the line of succession was born.

According to custom, Mary withdrew from public life in early April to await the birth of her child. She had chosen Hampton Court as the stage of her confinement because it was close to London. No one entered the Queen's private sanctum "except the women who serve her and who have the same duties as the court officials".[17] In early May, a rumour spread across the country that Mary had given birth to a healthy baby

"Harbour of honourable gentlewomen"

boy. People of England rejoiced, wine ran freely through the streets and bonfires were lit. The rumour had even reached the courts of Charles V and Joanna of Austria, who both rejoiced and sent congratulatory letters. Yet it was a false alarm. The expected delivery date came and went, and still no baby was born.

Physicians were summoned to confer with the Queen, and they reached a verdict that she miscalculated her due date and the child was now expected to be born before 6 June 1555. "Everything in this kingdom depends on the Queen's safe deliverance", mused Simon Renard in a letter to Charles V. Yet no baby was born by 6 June. Whereas some Spaniards expressed doubts about the Queen's condition, Renard was hopeful. On 24 June, he informed the emperor that Mary's "doctors and ladies have proved to be out in their calculations by about two months, and it now appears that she will not be delivered before eight or ten days from now".[18] His comment reveals that the Queen's ladies-in-waiting were very much involved in the preparations and possessed valuable knowledge as to the state of Mary's intimate health.

The Queen, who remained a virgin until she married Philip at the age of thirty-seven, had little practical knowledge about sex or conception, so she had to rely on her physicians and the ladies of the Privy Chamber. As time went on and no baby was born, most people, except the Queen herself, lost hope that she was pregnant at all. Libel and malicious rumours spread across the country. Some claimed that "this rumour of the Queen's conception was spread by policy" while others believed she was "deceived by a tympany [distension of the abdomen] or some other like disease". There were also those who believed the Queen was pregnant but miscarried, and some even thought she was "bewitched".[19] Today historians believe that she had experienced phantom pregnancy.

As the weeks passed and nothing happened, the foreign diplomats approached the Queen's ladies-in-waiting to learn more. Antoine de Noailles, the French ambassador, learned from the Queen's midwife and one of her chief ladies that Mary was not pregnant because she had often sat on the floor of her chamber with knees drawn up to her chin, a position no pregnant woman could endure without considerable pain. Midwives and physicians were fearful to tell Mary the truth, and so she continued in her false hope.[20]

Even the most trusted among the Queen's servants, Susan Clarencius, flattered Mary's hopes. An anonymous contemporary writer condemned Susan and other ladies who assured Mary that she was with child. He related "how Mrs Clarencius and divers others, as parasites about her, assured her to be with child, insomuch as the Queen was fully so persuaded herself".[21] Only one lady, Frideswide Strelley, was bold enough to express doubts about the Queen's condition. At

"Harbour of honourable gentlewomen"

some point, when she herself started doubting whether she was with child, Mary sent for Frideswide and declared: "Ah, Strelley, Strelley, I see they be all flatterers, and none true to me but thou." After this incident, Strelley was more favoured than ever before.[22]

By August 1555, the Queen showed no signs of pregnancy, and she had moved on with her life. Her husband left England on 29 August, and Mary bid him farewell and appeared outwardly calm, but when she reached her private apartments, she gave vent to her real feelings. Sitting by the window overlooking the river and watching her husband sail away, she burst into tears. Abandoned by her beloved Philip, rendered unpopular by the persecution of heretics and surrounded by treachery on a daily basis, the Queen soon succumbed to depression. Giacomo Soranzo, the Venetian diplomat, observed that Mary was prone to "a very deep melancholy".[23] Frequent bloodletting, caused by irregular menstruations, rendered her "pale and emaciated". Childlessness pained Mary the most since she feared that her half sister, Elizabeth, an heiress apparent, would undo all her religious policies and turn away from the Catholic Church as their father did. The Queen wrote letter after letter to her absent husband, pouring her heart out in an attempt to induce him to return to England. Philip wrote back that he would return if she promised to crown him. Disillusioned, Mary told her ladies that she intended to "withdraw utterly from men, and live quietly, as she had done the chief part of her life before she married".[24]

Philip finally returned to Mary in March 1557, but he was not motivated by love; he needed her support in a war against France and the papacy. Mary, ever eager to please him, yielded to his wishes. In the eyes of her subjects, this was the most disastrous decision of her entire reign since it resulted in England losing Calais, its last outpost in France. Philip departed once more, this time never to see Mary again, though she was hopeful about being pregnant. When Pedro de Ocaña, a Spanish diplomat, had an audience with the Queen on 25 February 1558, he reported that she was with child and lived in confinement, but it was not until Susan Clarencius informed him that the Queen "will be delivered sometime this month or early in March" that he was sure.[25] This dispatch shows that Susan was still in the Queen's good graces despite the fact that she was condemned for abetting Mary in her mistaken belief in 1555. It is possible that Susan truly believed her royal mistress to have been with child in 1555 and then again in 1558. Despite having been married, there is no record of Susan having any children. When she composed her last will in 1557, she made her nephews and other family members her heirs. It is possible that she was equally ignorant as the Queen when it came to conception and pregnancy.

"Harbour of honourable gentlewomen"

The symptoms Mary mistook for pregnancy were in fact the early signs of a disease—possibly ovarian cancer—that killed her several months later. It soon became apparent that the Queen was not pregnant but mortally ill. Shivering and feverish, lying in her darkened bedchamber surrounded by a handful of trusted ladies-in-waiting, Mary had to come to terms with the thought of Elizabeth succeeding her. Despite praising her half sister to their father when Elizabeth was a small child, Mary had come to detest her younger sibling. Elizabeth had Henry VIII's flaming red hair and hooked nose, but her face and deportment reminded Mary of Anne Boleyn. Twenty-two years after Anne's execution, Mary still harboured hurtful memories. She could not accept Anne's daughter on the throne. Mary had once told the Venetian ambassador that Elizabeth "was born of an infamous woman who had so greatly outraged the Queen her mother and herself", and she was not about to let someone like Elizabeth govern the nation.[26] The worst thing about Elizabeth in Mary's view was that, much like Anne Boleyn, she had "a power of enchantment".[27] Every time Mary confronted her, Elizabeth made a show of obedience, begging Mary to be her good sister and sovereign. The main difference between them was that Mary could not pretend and Elizabeth was a consummate actress. The Queen, increasingly bitter as her hopes for a child were becoming ever more distant, created this illusion that Elizabeth was not Henry VIII's daughter but "had the face and countenance of Mark Smeaton", who was executed as one of Anne Boleyn's putative lovers in 1536.[28] If Elizabeth was not really her half sister, it was easier to loathe her and remove her from succession altogether. But Mary never made that step, perhaps because deep down she knew Elizabeth was a Tudor.

Later in her life, Elizabeth would reminisce about her half sister's last moments and recall how the fickle nobles and diplomats all flocked to her household to pay their respects to her as if the Queen were already dead. Mary was all but buried alive, and only the most trusted of her servants remained at her side. One of them was twenty-year-old Jane Dormer, a Catholic maid of honour who worshipped her royal mistress. Looking back at her young days in Mary's service, Jane would reflect that Mary's court was "the only harbour for honourable young gentlewomen, given any way to piety and devotion" and "the true school of virtuous demeanour, befitting the education that ought to be in noble damsels".[29] Jane was one of Mary's favourite servants; she slept in the Queen's bedchamber, read books and religious texts to her, cared for her jewels and personal belongings and was a carver at the Queen's table. Mary would often talk to Jane about her turbulent childhood, recalling her mother's advice and piety, as well as reliving the moments of humiliation she endured

"Harbour of honourable gentlewomen"

when Anne Boleyn was her father's wife. Jane preserved these memories in the pages of her memoir.

Jane was very young when she first entered the Queen's service, and she had literally grown up in the atmosphere of Mary's pious household. Her name appears in Mary's establishment before 1553, the year of her accession, so Jane witnessed a great deal of Mary's life prior to her coronation. Jane's youth, her beauty and devotion to the Queen marked her out as suitable bride material, but she rejected many suitors, or so she claimed in her memoir. "Jane Dormer deserved a very good husband" was the Queen's favourite saying, and she often added that "she knew not the man that was worthy of her".[30] Jane later reminisced that the Queen treated her more as if she were her mother or sister and not her royal mistress.

Despite the fact that an anonymous Spaniard asserted that Mary's ladies were unattractive and that "not a single Spanish gentleman has fallen in love with one of them nor takes any interest in them", Jane Dormer found a suitor in the person of Gómez Suárez de Figueroa y Córdoba, Count (later Duke) of Feria. The Queen wanted to be present at the couple's wedding after Philip's return from Flanders, but Philip's absence and her grave illness made it impossible. Lying ill in her bed and continually served by the loyal Jane, Mary realised she would not be present at her favourite maid of honour's

Great Ladies

wedding. In her last moments, the Queen did not think about herself but about the women who dedicated their lives to her service:

"She comforted those of them that grieved about her; she told them what good dreams she had, seeing many little children like angels play before her, singing pleasing notes, giving her more than earthly comfort; and thus persuaded all, ever to have the holy fear of God before their eyes, which would free them from all evil, and be a curb to all temptation. She asked them to think that whatsoever came to them was by God's permission; and ever to have confidence that He would in mercy turn all to the best."[31]

Mary retained "quickness of her senses and memory" until her last breath, and just before she died, she ordered Jane Dormer to be the one to tell Elizabeth that she was now Queen. After her royal mistress's death, Jane went to Elizabeth and bequeathed Mary's precious jewels to her, as was the late Queen's dying wish. She also gave Elizabeth instructions from Mary "to uphold and continue Catholic religion, to be good to her servants, and to pay what might justly be required". Reminiscing about these events later in her life, Jane scoffed at Elizabeth's pretended change of religious views. During Mary's reign, Elizabeth converted to Catholicism, and whenever her devotion was doubted by the Queen, she "prayed God that the earth might open and swallow her up alive" if she was not a

"Harbour of honourable gentlewomen"

good Roman Catholic.[32] She dropped the pretence upon her accession.

After Mary's death on 17 November 1558, Jane Dormer removed to her grandmother's rented lodgings at the Savoy Palace and on 29 December married the Count of Feria, who was thirty-eight at the time. The count left London on a diplomatic mission in the spring of 1559, and Jane was to follow him later that summer. In July 1559, seven months pregnant, the Countess of Feria had her last audience with Elizabeth. The Queen, whether deliberately or not, was late to the audience, and the Spanish ambassador loudly complained that she kept a heavily pregnant woman waiting in the summer heat. Elizabeth was later angry with the ambassador, but she had a "very much familiar and loving talk" with Jane.[33] By the time of her departure, Jane had a large household of her own, with six ladies who tended to her every need. Among the women who left for Spain in her entourage were Jane's grandmother and Susan Clarencius, Mary Tudor's faithful servant. Susan and Jane had developed a strong friendship, and Jane apparently felt responsible for the late Queen's favourite lady, who had no immediate family.

Jane Dormer's journey started in Dover, where she took leave of her family. From thence she travelled through Calais, Graveling, Dunkirk, Newport, Bruges, Ghent, Antwerp and Liege, before reaching Malines, where she intended to give birth. At each stop, she received a semi-regal welcome. On 14 October 1559, she gave birth to her son, Lorenzo, but fell sick shortly afterwards and was unable to resume the journey. On 5 November, the Count of Feria wrote to the Bishop of Aquila that his wife was "still sadly ailing, but the boy is well". The count's letter reveals that Susan Clarencius had "the entire care of the child" and was "wonderfully attentive".[34]

In the same letter, the Count of Feria implored the Bishop of Aquila to make sure that Susan and "the old Lady Dormer", Jane's beloved grandmother, received licences from Queen Elizabeth. Apparently, the ladies left England without taking their official leave of Mary's successor. Susan appears to have prepared well for the journey ahead since she made sure that her nephews received her lands and other property. But without obtaining a licence from Elizabeth, her property stood at risk of being confiscated. Elizabeth threw certain impediments in the way, and in March 1560 the Count of Feria took it as a "great unkindness that the Queen denied him licence for the Lady Dormer's longer tarrying here and for Clarencius's going into Spain".[35] It seems that Elizabeth took offence that the ladies did not seek her permission before they left. It was unacceptable that Susan Clarencius, the chief lady of her half sister's Privy Chamber, left without farewell. This strongly suggests that Susan and Elizabeth were on bad terms

"Harbour of honourable gentlewomen"

during Mary's reign, and that there was no affection between them.

Mary's reign was the darkest period in Elizabeth's life. "I stood in danger of my life, my sister was so incensed against me", Elizabeth reminded her councillors when they pressed her to name a successor.[36] Elizabeth harboured resentment against Mary even after the latter's death, but she refrained from speaking ill of her. Even if the cause of the ill treatment lay with Mary, Elizabeth sighed, "I will not now burden her therewith because I will not charge the dead".[37] But she could charge Mary's faithful servants. In late 1560, Elizabeth wrote to King Philip, Mary's former husband, that the elderly ladies Dormer and Clarencius would retain her favour if only they returned to England and lived quietly ever after. Yet the women had no intention of returning to Elizabethan England and never obtained their licences. Susan was retained in the Feria household until the end of her life. The exact date of her death is not recorded, but she was dead by the spring of 1564.

NOTES

[1] *Calendar of State Papers, Spain,* Volume 11, entry for 17 November 1553.
[2] John Foxe, *Actes and Monuments,* Volume 10 pp. 148-9.
[3] John Gough Nichols, *The Chronicle of Queen Jane and of Two Years of Queen Mary,* pp. 128-9.
[4] Ibid.

Great Ladies

[5] Nicholas Harris Nicolas, *Memoirs and Literary Remains of Lady Jane Grey*, p. 47.

[6] John Gough Nichols, *The Chronicle of Queen Jane and of Two Years of Queen Mary*, p. 59.

[7] Ibid., p. 56.

[8] *Calendar of State Papers, Spain,* Volume 13, 1554-1558, entry for 2 October 1554.

[9] Ibid., entry for 17 August 1554.

[10] *Calendar of State Papers, Venice,* Volume 5, n. 934.

[11] *Calendar of State Papers, Spain,* Volume 13, 1554-1558, entry for 10 December 1554.

[12] Ibid., entry for 2 October 1554.

[13] Ibid.

[14] Ibid., entry for 12 August 1554.

[15] *Calendar of State Papers, Venice,* Volume 6, n. 882.

[16] *Calendar of State Papers, Spain,* Volume 13, 1554-1558, entry for 29 July 1554.

[17] Ibid., entry for 21 April 1555.

[18] Ibid., entry for 24 June 1555.

[19] John Foxe, *The Actes and Monuments*, Volume 7, p. 126.

[20] Abbe de Vertot, *Ambassades de Messieurs de Noailles en Angleterre,* Volume 4, pp. 334-5.

[21] J.M. Stone, *The History of Mary I*, pp. 350-1.

[22] Ibid.

[23] *Calendar of State Papers, Venice,* Volume 6, n. 882.

[24] Ibid., n. 332.

[25] *Calendar of State Papers, Spain,* Volume 13, 1554-1558, entry for 25 February 1558.

[26] *Calendar of State Papers, Venice,* Volume 6, n. 1274.

[27] *Calendar of State Papers, Spain,* Volume 11, entry for 9 September 1553.

[28] Henry Clifford, *The Life of Jane Dormer, Duchess of Feria*, p. 80.

[29] Ibid., p. 63.

[30] Ibid., p. 68.

[31] Ibid., p. 70.

[32] Ibid., pp. 72-3.

[33] *Calendar of State Papers Foreign: Elizabeth*, Volume 1, n. 1082.

[34] *Calendar of State Papers, Spain (Simancas),* Volume 1, 1558-1567, n. 71.

[35] *Calendar of State Papers Foreign: Elizabeth*, Volume 2, 1559-1560, n. 838.

"Harbour of honourable gentlewomen"

---

[36] Clark Hulse, *Elizabeth I: Ruler and Legend*, p. 26.

[37] John Nichols, *The Progresses and Public Processions of Queen Elizabeth*, Volume 1, p. 64.

CHAPTER 17
"HER MOST INTIMATE LADY OF THE BEDCHAMBER"

"The kingdom is entirely in the hands of young folks, heretics and traitors", proclaimed the outraged Count of Feria shortly after Elizabeth's accession. Feria remained in England after Mary's death to represent his master and the late Queen's widower, King Philip. Feria held several audiences with Elizabeth before and after Mary's death, and he formed a strong opinion about the new Queen's character. "She is a very strange sort of woman", he wrote in one of his dispatches, adding that she was vain and well-schooled in the way her father had ruled.[1] The reason behind his judgment was Elizabeth's self-confidence and unwillingness to be guided by anyone. Feria observed that she was "highly indignant about what has been done to her during the Queen's lifetime". In consequence, Elizabeth did not "favour a single man whom Her Majesty, who is now in heaven, would have received and will take no one into her service who served her sister when she was Lady Mary".

"Her most intimate Lady of the Bedchamber"

This was also true when it came to the late Queen's ladies-in-waiting. Most of them were dismissed and left court, although there were some notable exceptions. Anne Reade and Barbara Hawk, who served in Mary's household for years, were rewarded. Reade owed her post as lady-in-waiting in Elizabeth's household to her relationship to the Boleyn family while Hawk received gowns from Elizabeth on at least two occasions, perhaps for services rendered during Mary's reign.[2]

In stark contrast to her half sister, Elizabeth left the past behind and never proclaimed herself to be a legitimate daughter of Henry VIII and Anne Boleyn. During Mary's reign, Elizabeth was reviled as a daughter of an adulteress, yet she entertained a high opinion of her executed mother. In 1557, the Venetian ambassador recorded that Elizabeth was "proud and haughty as although she knows that she was born of such a mother, she nevertheless does not consider herself of inferior degree to the Queen, whom she equals in self-esteem; nor does she believe herself less legitimate than her Majesty, alleging in her own favour that her mother would never cohabit with the King unless by way of marriage, with the authority of the Church, and the intervention of the Primate of England". Yet despite her high opinion of Anne Boleyn, Elizabeth "prides herself on her father and glories in him; everybody saying that she also resembles him more than the Queen does".[3] Throughout her reign, Elizabeth drew parallels between herself and her illustrious father. She was the "lion's cub", and despite having a body "of a weak and feeble woman", she had "the heart and stomach [courage] of a king".[4]

Elizabeth derived her claim to the throne directly from her royal father, and she glorified him in public. In the presence chamber at Hampton Court, under the canopy of estate, "Long Live King Henry VIII" was sewn together from pearls. In the hall, Elizabeth kept a portrait of her father with a Holy Bible displayed underneath. The portrait of Anne Boleyn was sadly missing, but there were other artefacts belonging to Anne in Elizabeth's palaces. According to the German visitor Paul Hentzner, who travelled through England when Elizabeth was an old woman in 1598, there was a special chamber in Windsor Castle "in which are the royal beds of Henry VII and his Queen, of Edward VI, of Henry VIII, and of Anne Boleyn, all of them eleven feet square, and covered with quilts shining with gold and silver". Near Elizabeth's bedchamber at Hampton Court, Hentzner continued, "we were shown a bed, the tester [covering for the bed-head] of which was worked by Anne Boleyn, and presented by her to her husband Henry VIII".[5]

Elizabeth had also surrounded herself with her mother's relatives and was glad to place them near her. "All the heretics who had escaped are beginning to flock back again from Germany", noticed the Count of Feria in early

"Her most intimate Lady of the Bedchamber"

December 1558.[6] Among them were Elizabeth's relatives: Katherine Knollys, with her husband and children, and Katherine's stepmother, Dorothy Stafford. Born as Katherine Carey in the early 1520s, Katherine was the only daughter of Mary Carey, Anne Boleyn's sister. She had a younger brother named Henry, who was born on 4 March 1526 and who was rumoured to have been Henry VIII's son.[7] Whether one or both of Mary's children were fathered by Henry VIII when she was his mistress remains unknown but plausible; a portrait of Katherine painted when she was thirty-eight shows a remarkable resemblance to the King.[8] Whether the Careys were Elizabeth's half siblings or first cousins, they were her closest family members and highly esteemed by the Queen. When Katherine left for exile during the reign of Mary Tudor, Elizabeth signed her farewell letter to her as "Cor Rotto" or "Broken Heart". Elizabeth certainly acknowledged the blood tie between them and addressed Katherine as her "loving cousin and ready friend".[9]

Just how and when they became such close friends remains unknown. Katherine, whose date of birth is usually placed c. 1524, was at least nine years older than Elizabeth. She may have been placed in Elizabeth's early household—if so, then she served there since Elizabeth's birth in 1533 until Katherine's marriage to Francis Knollys in 1540. From 1541 to 1562, Katherine was occupied with almost annual

Great Ladies

childbearing. Two of her children—Katherine and Dudley— were born during Elizabeth's reign, and the latter was named after the Queen's great favourite, Robert Dudley.[10] Katherine and her entire family found employment at Elizabeth's court immediately after the Queen's accession. Katherine became one of the chief Gentlewomen of the Bedchamber while her beautiful daughter, the fifteen-year-old Lettice, joined the Privy Chamber.[11]

The second wife of Katherine's father, Dorothy Stafford, also found a prestigious post in Elizabeth's household. Born in 1526, Dorothy was the granddaughter of Margaret Pole, Countess of Salisbury, and a widow of William Stafford, Mary Carey's beloved second husband. William Stafford died in 1553 and never saw Elizabeth ascend the throne. Dorothy had several children with him and never remarried after his death. Her epitaph recorded that "she served Queen Elizabeth for forty years, lying in the Bedchamber, esteemed of her".[12]

Beyond her maternal relatives, Elizabeth also employed a number of women who had served her since her early childhood. It has been speculated that some of these women were appointed by Anne Boleyn, but this seems unlikely. When Blanche Herbert, Lady Herbert of Troy, who served as one of the governesses to royal children, recommended the wet nurse who would breastfeed the

"Her most intimate Lady of the Bedchamber"

princess, it was remarked that Anne Boleyn would have chosen this candidate if she "had her own will therein".[13] This incident shows that whereas Anne had no say in who would breastfeed her own child, she worked closely with the royal governess. Blanche evidently stood high in Anne's favour if she was allowed to recommend a wet nurse for Elizabeth. Blanche's name also figures in the 1534 New Year's gift roll and in the list of Anne Boleyn's debts in 1536, which is additional proof that the two women shared a close relationship. Blanche Herbert was an aunt and godmother of Blanche Parry, who served as a rocker of Elizabeth's cradle. Blanche Herbert died before Elizabeth's accession, but her niece became the Queen's servant and one of her favourites. Parry provided a precious link to Anne Boleyn; she certainly could and did pass many stories about the mother Elizabeth never knew.

The woman Elizabeth felt especially bound to was her governess, Katherine "Kat" Champernowne, who joined Elizabeth's household in the autumn of 1536. Ironically, Kat owed her appointment to Thomas Cromwell, the man who had engineered Anne Boleyn's downfall only months earlier.[14] In 1545, Kat married Elizabeth's distant relative, John Ashley, whose royal service hearkened back to the time when Anne Boleyn was Queen.[15] Kat stood by Elizabeth through thick and thin, and Elizabeth later recalled that Kat took a "great labour

Great Ladies

and pain in bringing of me up in learning and honesty". She also added that "St Gregory sayeth that we are more bound to them that bringeth us up well than to our parents, for our parents do that which is natural for them—that is, bringeth us into this world—but our bringers-up are a cause to make us live well in it".[16] There is no doubt that Kat was a mother figure to Elizabeth and that she was the only person who could reprimand her royal mistress and get away with it.

From the earliest days of Elizabeth's reign, courtiers and ambassadors were exchanging scandalous rumours about the Queen's relationship with her Master of the Horse, Robert Dudley.[17] In April 1559, the Count of Feria wrote: "During the last few days Lord Robert has come so much into favour that he does whatever he likes with affairs and it is even said that her Majesty visits him in his chamber day and night."[18] Those at court who resented Dudley's influence over the Queen spread rumours that his wife had "a malady in one of her breasts and the Queen is only waiting for her to die to marry Lord Robert".[19]

Many believed that Elizabeth was not a virgin and that her relationship with Robert was sexual in nature. The celebration of Elizabeth's virginity did not start until the 1580s, when it became apparent that she would never marry. In the early years of her reign, however, Elizabeth was regularly pestered by her councillors on the matter, and it is

"Her most intimate Lady of the Bedchamber"

clear that even Kat Ashley, who knew Elizabeth's aversion to marriage, desired to convince the Queen that her primary duty was to marry and bear children. One day, Kat knelt in front of the Queen and urged her to change her behaviour. The emperor's ambassador, Baron Caspar Breuner, reported the incident:

"Her most intimate Lady of the Bedchamber, Katherine Ashley, some days ago fell at Her Majesty's feet, and on being questioned, implored her in God's name to marry and put an end to all these disreputable rumours, telling Her Majesty that her behaviour towards the said Master of the Horse occasioned much evil-speaking; for she showed herself so affectionate to him that Her Majesty's honour and dignity would be sullied, and her subjects would in time become discontented. Her Majesty would thus be the cause of much bloodshed in this realm, for which she would have to give account to God and by which she would merit the eternal curse of her subjects. Rather than that this should happen she would have strangled Her Majesty in the cradle."[20]

Elizabeth, who was famous for her volatile temper, did not upbraid Kat but replied that she knew Kat's words were a reflection of her "true fidelity" to her royal mistress. The Queen informed Kat that she would consider marrying, but at present she had no intention of taking a husband. As to her relationship with Robert Dudley, Elizabeth said that she had "never understood how any single person could be displeased, seeing that she was always surrounded by her Ladies of the Bedchamber and Maids-of-Honour, who at all times could see whether there was anything dishonourable between her and her Master of the Horse". She also added that "if she had ever had the will or had found pleasure in such a dishonourable life . . . she did not know of anyone who could forbid her; but she trusted in God that nobody would ever live to see her so commit herself".[21]

Elizabeth acknowledged that the constant presence of her ladies-in-waiting was a safeguard to her reputation: She was under their scrutiny from the moment she rose in the morning until she got undressed late at night. They knew everything about their Queen—her habits, quirks, whether she menstruated regularly and when she had trouble sleeping at night. "My life is in the open, and I have so many witnesses that I cannot understand how so bad a judgment can have been formed of me", she complained to the Spanish ambassador in 1564.[22]

The woman who was so eager to protect Elizabeth's reputation died on 18 July 1565. Kat Ashley's death was unexpected, and the Queen was beset with grief. The Spanish ambassador Guzman De Silva recorded that Elizabeth visited Kat the day before she died and "greatly grieved" after her passing.[23] Kat's position as chief Gentlewoman of the Privy

"Her most intimate Lady of the Bedchamber"

Chamber was quickly filled by Blanche Parry, who now became the Queen's chief favourite. Although she could not know it at the time, Blanche was to become the longest-serving among Elizabeth's women.

NOTES

[1] *Calendar of State Papers, Spain (Simancas),* Volume 1, 1558-1567, n. 4.

[2] Charlotte Merton, *The Women Who Served Queen Mary and Queen Elizabeth*, p. 33.

[3] *Calendar of State Papers, Venice,* Volume 6, n. 882.

[4] *Queen Elizabeth's Tilbury speech,* July 1588, *British Library's Learning Timelines: Sources from History* [http://www.bl.uk/learning/timeline/item102878.html]

[5] Paul Hentzner, *Travels in England*, pp. 56-7.

[6] *Calendar of State Papers, Spain (Simancas),* Volume 1, n. 4.

[7] During his trial in 1535, John Hale, Vicar of Isleworth, confessed that: "Mr Skidmore did show me young Master Carey, saying that he was our sovereign lord the King's son by our sovereign lady the Queen's sister, whom the Queen's grace might not suffer to be in the Court". *Letters and Papers, Henry VIII,* Volume 8, n. 567.

[8] Pauline Croft and Karen Hearn, "Only matrimony maketh children to be certain..." Two Elizabethan pregnancy portraits, *The British Art Journal,* Vol. 3, No. 3 (Autumn 2002), pp. 19-24.

[9] Maria Perry, *The Word of a Prince: A Life of Elizabeth I from Contemporary Documents*, p. 58.

[10] Sally Varlow, *Sir Francis Knollys's Latin Dictionary: New Evidence for Katherine Carey*, p. 9.

[11] BL Landsowne MS 3, f. 193.

[12] Quoted from Dorothy Stafford's epitaph, St Margaret's Church, London, UK.

[13] *Calendar of the Cecil Papers in Hatfield House,* Volume 11, entry for 20 March 1601.

[14] *Letters and Papers, Foreign and Domestic, Henry VIII,* Volume 11, n. 639.

[15] He was the son of Anne Ashley, sister-in-law of James Boleyn, Anne Boleyn's paternal uncle. In 1536, Anne Boleyn loaned him a substantial sum of £100, indicative of a cordial relationship between them.

Great Ladies

[16] Leah S. Marcus, Janel Mueller, Mary Beth Rose, *Elizabeth I: Collected Works*, p. 34.

[17] He was the son of John Dudley, Duke of Northumberland.

[18] *Calendar of State Papers, Spain (Simancas)*, Volume 1, n. 27.

[19] Ibid.

[20] Victor von Klarwill (ed.), *Queen Elizabeth and Some Foreigners*, pp. 113-15.

[21] Ibid.

[22] *Calendar of State Papers, Spain (Simancas)*, Volume 1, 1558-1567, n. 270.

[23] Ibid., n. 310.

CHAPTER 18
"IN THE PRINCE'S COURT"

The competition among women who aspired to become Queen Elizabeth's ladies-in-waiting was fierce. A charming anecdote exists about how a young noblewoman started her career at court. On 1 January 1561, New Year's Day, Humphrey Radcliffe "brought forward his daughter Mary and laughingly presented her as a New Year's gift". The amused Queen accepted this unusual gift and appointed Mary as one of her numerous maids of honour.[1] This anecdote shows just how coveted a position as the Queen's female servant was.

Yet being Queen Elizabeth's woman had its dark side too. Maids of honour—young, beautiful and marriageable—often lived in appalling conditions and were the object of ribald attention. At Windsor, their quarters were so primitive that they petitioned "to have their chamber ceiled, and the partition that is of boards there to be made higher, for that the servants look over".[2] Luxury and pomp surrounded the Queen everywhere she went, but the same cannot be said of her women's accommodations. Greenwich Palace and other stately houses were often filled "with such savours, as where many mouths be fed can hardly be avoided".[3] Yet it was not the luxury of life that attracted women to Elizabeth's service—it was Elizabeth herself. She was the font of all patronage, and women did all they could to stay in her good graces.

Yet sometimes even the ladies who proved their loyalty to the Queen suffered from her neglect. Mary Sidney, one of the sisters of Robert Dudley, enjoyed a close relationship with Elizabeth and nursed her when the Queen fell sick with smallpox in 1562. The Queen, who was very attached to her appearance, regained her health and was lucky to escape with not "many signs in her face".[4] Mary Sidney was not so lucky; she had caught smallpox while devotedly nursing Elizabeth, and although she recovered, she was badly disfigured with unsightly pockmarks. "When I went to Newhaven I left her a full fair lady, in mine eye, at least, the fairest", wrote her husband, adding that "when I returned I found her as foul a lady as the smallpox could make her".[5]

Elizabeth hated any reminders of her near-deadly sickness and never showed Mary the gratitude she deserved for the service she performed at the peril of her own life. Mary was an unsalaried member of the Queen's household and relied on Elizabeth's charity. At the same time, Mary was entitled to free board and lodgings at court, and the Queen had the right to summon her whenever she liked. In 1574, after a brief absence from court, Mary was forced to ask for a loan of "three or four lined pieces of hanging" for her chamber to

"In the prince's court"

prevent draughts since "Her Majesty had commanded me to come to the court and my chamber is very cold and my own hangings very scant and nothing warm".[6]

Ladies who surrounded the Queen on a daily basis and tended to her needs in private had a rare chance to observe Elizabeth and form judgments about her personality. The Queen was notoriously jealous of her young and beautiful female servants and made sure that none of them upstaged her. She was often fishing for compliments and once asked a French nobleman what he thought of her ladies. Knowing Elizabeth was notoriously vain, he replied that he could not possibly "judge stars in the presence of the sun".[7]

As time went by and Elizabeth grew older, it became obvious that she would never marry and have children. Among her most favourite ladies was Blanche Parry, who decided to follow the Queen's example and remain a virgin, but other women were not so willing to eschew matrimony. Some of the women at court married behind the Queen's back and experienced the full force of her wrath. Women such as Katherine and Mary Grey, who married without royal consent, were banished from court, dying in obscurity. Others, like the Queen's distant cousin and favourite maid, Mary Shelton, were pardoned for marrying but had to endure Elizabeth's fiery outbursts. Mary approached the Queen and asked for permission to marry Sir John Scudamore, but Elizabeth exploded in anger and broke Mary's finger, later trying to blame the injury on a falling candlestick. She later pardoned Mary and promoted her to a prestigious position in the Privy Chamber, but Mary's friend, Eleanor Bridges, remarked that no one had ever bought a husband more dearly than Mary, who received "blows and evil words" from their royal mistress.[8]

Elizabeth had a fiery temper and often threw tantrums, breaking cups and bowls and inflicting physical punishment on her ladies. The ambassadors who dealt with her emphasized that she was arrogant, coarse and narcissistic. She had a habit "to make long digressions and after much circumlocution to come to the point of which she wishes to speak". She often swore and blasphemed "grievously by God and by Christ" and berated her councillors and ladies in strong language.[9] "When she smiled, it was a pure sunshine that everyone did choose to bask in if they could", wrote the Queen's godson John Harrington, "but anon came a storm from a sudden gathering of clouds, and the thunder fell in wondrous manner on all alike".[10] Elizabeth often mistreated even those women whom she favoured. Francis Knollys, the husband of Katherine, wrote to his beloved wife that "for the outward love that her Majesty bears you, she makes you often weep for unkindness to the great danger of your health".[11] The foreign

"In the prince's court"

ambassadors remarked that the Queen often swore at her ladies and even resorted to beating them.[12]

Elizabeth was also very possessive, and once she took a liking to one of her women, she refused to let them go. When Katherine Knollys fell gravely ill, her husband, who served as custodian of the imprisoned Mary Queen of Scots, petitioned the Queen to be allowed to return to London and visit his wife. Elizabeth refused. When Katherine's health improved, she begged the Queen to allow her to join her husband in the remote north, but Elizabeth refused again, arguing that the long journey might endanger Katherine's fragile health. Francis Knollys was outraged, and he wrote a long letter wherein he told his beloved wife that he would be glad to retire from court with her and lead a "country poor life". Katherine never replied to her husband's loving letter; she died on 15 January 1569 at Hampton Court. Nicholas White, one of William Cecil's emissaries, described how the Queen grieved after her kinswoman's death:

"From this she returned back again to talk of my Lady Knollys. And after many speeches to and fro of that gentlewoman, I perceiving her to harp much upon her departure, said that the long absence of her husband . . . together with the fervency of her fever, did greatly further her end, wanting nothing else that either art or man's help could devise for her recovery, lying in the prince's court near her

Great Ladies

person, where every hour her careful ear understood of her estate, and where also she was very often visited by Her Majesty's comfortable presence."[13]

White further added that "although her Grace was not culpable of this accident, yet she was the cause, without which their being asunder had not happened". Elizabeth was not about to make any excuses; she simply said "she was very sorry" for Katherine Knollys's death.[14] The only thing the Queen could do was to pay for a lavish funeral and take care of her kinswoman's children. Katherine was buried in Westminster Abbey, where a coloured alabaster monument near her grave still stands today as a silent reminder of her selfless service as "the chief Lady of the Queen's Majesty's Bedchamber".[15]

NOTES

[1] Violet A. Wilson, *Queen Elizabeth's Maids of Honour and Ladies of the Privy Chamber*, p. 41.

[2] *The Civil Engineer and Architect's Journal*, Volume 4, p. 279.

[3] Sir John Harington, *The Metamorphosis of Ajax*, p. 7.

[4] *Calendar of State Papers, Foreign, Elizabeth*, n. 1053.

[5] *Calendar of the Carew Manuscripts*, ed. Brewer, Bullen, p. 9.

[6] Margaret P. Hannay, *Philip's Phoenix: Mary Sidney, Countess of Pembroke*, p. 30.

[7] Violet A. Wilson, *Queen Elizabeth's Maids of Honour*, p. 3.

[8] *The Manuscripts of His Grace the Duke of Rutland, G.C.B., Preserved at Belvoir Castle*, Volume 1, p. 107.

[9] Victor Klarwill, *Queen Elizabeth and Some Foreigners*, p. 145.

[10] Sir John Harington, *Nugae Antiquae*, Volume 2, p. 140-41.

[11] Susan Doran, *Elizabeth I and Her Circle*, p. 122.

"In the prince's court"

[12] Ibid.

[13] Henry Alfred Napier, *Historical Notices of the Parishes of Swycombe and Ewelme*, p. 370.

[14] Ibid.

[15] Quoted from the inscription on Katherine's monument: [http://www.westminster-abbey.org/our history/people/katherine-knollys]

CHAPTER 19
"SUCH A SHE WOLF"

Despite the fact that Elizabeth communicated her decision never to marry to her subjects in the early days of her reign, rumours about her alleged affairs and supposed pregnancies circulated in England throughout her life. People wanted to peer inside her body to see if she was with child, and every indisposition bore rumours about the state of her intimate health. Although Elizabeth was annoyed by such slurs, she often fuelled them herself. Her relationship with Robert Dudley was way too informal for the sensitive moral standards of the sixteenth century. Dudley was the only man who could unceremoniously enter the Queen's private sanctum, her bedchamber. Often indisposed, Elizabeth spent a great deal of time in her bedchamber, frequently receiving audiences there. Unlike her royal male predecessors—her grandfather, father and brother—Elizabeth could not invite her councillors to come into her private apartments without at least an hour of notice. As a woman, she had to guard her privacy and prepare for visitors, especially if they were men. In the masculine world of Henry VIII, men could often come in unannounced to the King's bedchamber to discuss politics, but such liberty was unthinkable during Elizabeth's reign.

"Such a She Wolf"

Robert Dudley, however, was treated in a special way. He was criticised by courtiers jealous of his influence for entering the Queen's bedchamber before she rose and for taking "upon himself the office of her lady-in-waiting by handing her a garment which ought never to have been seen in the hands of her Master of the Horse".[1] He also kissed Elizabeth without being invited to do so, a clear breach of etiquette. But Dudley could hardly have done all this without having the Queen's tacit approval. It is clear that the two shared a close relationship. With Dudley in her presence, Elizabeth could relax and become a private person and not the regal persona. Dudley knew her "better than any man" and entertained her with his impeccable sense of humour.[2] Elizabeth liked to shun formality whenever she could, and with Dudley she was free to laugh, joke and poke fun without appearing ridiculous. This lack of pompous formality in her contact with Dudley invited salacious gossip. Some dissatisfied nobles claimed that the Queen and Dudley held intimate meetings at the privy stairs leading to Elizabeth's suite and "if they had not used sorcery [means to prevent unwanted pregnancy], there should have been young traitors 'ere now begotten".[3] The scandalous gossip proliferated, and there was nothing Elizabeth could do about it.

One way to end the speculations would have been to marry Robert Dudley, but despite the rumours of their evident

Great Ladies

closeness, Elizabeth never decided to do so. After his wife's mysterious death in 1560—Amy Dudley was found dead with a broken neck and two head injuries at the foot of the staircase of Cumnor Place in Oxfordshire—Robert was free to remarry. Whether out of ambition or love, Dudley nurtured hopes of becoming the Queen's husband until 1575, when he entertained her at his palace of Kenilworth, vigorously promoting his matrimonial suit. William Cecil had once mused that "carnal marriages begin in gladness and end in strife", and this was vividly proved by the experiences of Elizabeth's parents.[4] Henry VIII courted Anne Boleyn with tenderness, penning impassioned love letters and disrupting the religious and social order to make her his wife, only to discover that his sexual fascination with Anne waned shortly after their wedding. It is tempting to speculate that Elizabeth was afraid to lose Dudley's affection after the chase ended and wished to remain an unattainable, adored mistress to retain her allure over him. She did not expect that Dudley would one day give up on his hopes of marrying her. Fickle and unpredictable, Elizabeth regarded Dudley as her exclusive property, but Dudley—handsome, athletic and wealthy—was a magnet for women. He had nothing against occasional flings, as illustrated by his relationship with the beautiful Douglas Sheffield. On 7 August 1574, a year before Dudley invited Elizabeth to Kenilworth to renew his matrimonial suit, Douglas gave birth to Dudley's illegitimate son, who was named Robert after him.

"Such a She Wolf"

Douglas pressed Robert to marry her before their child's birth, but he was afraid that he might lose the Queen's affection if he remarried. Elizabeth was notoriously jealous, and when she discovered that Douglas and her sister "were at great wars together" because they were in love with Dudley, she "thinketh not well of them, and not the better of him" and put spies about Dudley.[5] Many years later, when Dudley and Elizabeth were dead, Dudley's son sought a share of his father's wealth, and Douglas testified that she and Dudley were clandestinely married in 1573. There was little evidence to prove this, and the case eventually collapsed. Dudley was convinced that his remarriage would lead to "mine utter overthrow", yet on 21 September 1578 he decided to risk Elizabeth's wrath and secretly married a woman with whom he had been in love for several years, Lettice Knollys.[6]

A daughter of the late Katherine Knollys, Lettice was the Queen's much-favoured kinswoman. In many respects, Lettice was a younger, healthier and more attractive version of Elizabeth. With her milky complexion, almond-shaped eyes and thick red locks, Lettice was judged to have been "one of the best-looking ladies of the court".[7] Dudley's relationship with Lettice started in 1565 when she was married to Walter Devereux, Earl of Essex. At that time, Dudley was advised to push Elizabeth into a decision to marry him by making her jealous, and so he started flirting with Lettice. After shedding

Great Ladies

many tears and upbraiding him "in very bitter words", Elizabeth reconciled with Dudley, although rumours about his secret liaison with Lettice persisted.[8]

Lettice's husband went to Ireland in 1573, and it appears that she continued her relationship with Dudley. She visited London on a regular basis, staying at Durham House, not far from Dudley's seat at Leicester House. She sometimes visited him at Kenilworth, where they enjoyed the nearby hunting grounds. By December 1575, when Lettice's husband returned from Ireland, her name was openly linked to Dudley's. According to the Spanish ambassador Antonio de Guarás, there was a "great enmity... between the Earl of Leicester and the Earl of Essex, in consequence, it is said, of the fact that whilst Essex was in Ireland his wife had two children by Leicester".[9] There were no children as yet, but the rumours rightly hinted at a close relationship between Lettice and Dudley.

Walter Devereux died of dysentery on 22 September 1576 in Dublin; it was later insinuated by malicious tongues that he was poisoned by Dudley. Two years later Dudley married Lettice in a secret ceremony. A reference to the "loose gown" Lettice wore on her wedding day led many authors to assume that she tricked Dudley into marrying her by informing him she was with child, but there is no doubt that she was not pregnant at the time, and Dudley married her for love.[10] This made it all the more painful for Elizabeth, who never forgave Lettice for what she perceived as stealing Dudley away from her.

The Queen was always agitated when she heard Lettice's name and described her as "such a she wolf" and "bad woman".[11] One hostile source asserted that when Lettice, dressed sumptuously and accompanied by a large train of servants, came to court soon after her marriage, the Queen boxed her ears, shouting: "As but one sun lights the East, so I shall have but one Queen of England." Rumours circulating in London at the time claimed that Lettice "vied in dress with the Queen" and lived in princely style, but this was all propaganda spread by Robert Dudley's enemies.[12] In truth, the Queen learned about Dudley's secret marriage over a year after the wedding took place. Dudley eventually regained the Queen's favour, but his wife was never allowed to return to court while he was alive and was forced to keep a low profile.

The Queen's enmity towards Lettice continued long after Robert Dudley's death. Robert, the only man Elizabeth truly loved, died in September 1588, not long after his part in defeating the Spanish Armada. His widow, drowning in debt, remarried within a year, but Elizabeth still hated her. Lettice's son from her first marriage, Robert Devereux, Earl of Essex, became the sweetheart of the Queen's declining years, and it was through his tireless mediation that Elizabeth agreed to an

Great Ladies

audience with the woman she hated so much. Despite the fact that the Queen agreed to see Lettice, she usually "found some occasion not to come" when her despised rival was hopefully awaiting the Queen in the privy galleries.

Finally, on 27 February 1597, Elizabeth decided to grant an audience to Lettice, who brought an exquisite jewel worth a staggering amount of £300 to pacify the Queen. An eyewitness to their meeting recorded that Lettice "kissed the Queen's hand and her breast, and embraced her, and the Queen kissed her".[13] Lettice was under the impression that all was well again and departed from court "exceedingly contented", but when she requested another audience, Elizabeth denied permission and used "some wonted unkind words" against her old rival.[14] This was to be the last meeting between the Queen and her kinswoman. Although Lettice's son was held in great favour by the Queen, he was disgraced in 1599. Essex, who was some thirty years Elizabeth's junior, knew that the Queen was vain and paid court to her in the chivalric tradition of courtly love. On one occasion, he burst into the Queen's bedchamber unannounced and saw Elizabeth in a state of disarray, without makeup and wig. The Queen made an imposing state figure in her sumptuous gowns, wigs and jewels, but beneath all that finery she was an old and infirm sixty-six-year-old human being. Essex later mocked the Queen as "an old woman . . . no less crooked in mind than in carcass".[15] Elizabeth never forgave Essex, and it was rumoured that this humiliating incident hastened the young earl's downfall.

When Lettice learned that her beloved son was disgraced and his life endangered, she was anxious to come "to Her Majesty's presence and kiss her hands". Lettice knew well that Elizabeth loved finery, and she sent her a "most curious fine gown" worth £100. The gown was presented by Mary Scudamore, one of the Queen's great favourites, and an eyewitness recorded that Elizabeth "liked it well", but she neither accepted it nor refused, commenting bitterly that "things standing as they did, it was not fit for her [Lettice] to desire what she did".[16]

Essex was briefly pardoned, but he never regained his former standing with the Queen and rebelled against her. To his mother's despair, he was executed on 25 February 1601. He was not the only casualty: Lettice's third husband, Christopher Blount, was also executed for his involvement in Essex's rebellion. Lettice never set foot in the Queen's chamber again.

NOTES

[1] Agnes Strickland, *Lives of the Queens of England*, p. 313.
[2] Anne Somerset, *Elizabeth I*, p. 55.
[3] Chris Skidmore, *Death and the Virgin*, Kindle edition.

Great Ladies

[4] Josephine Ross, *The Men Who Would Be King: Suitors to Queen Elizabeth I*, Kindle edition.

[5] Conyers Read, *A Letter from Robert, Earl of Leicester, to a Lady*, p. 18.

[6] Ibid., p. 24.

[7] *Calendar of State Papers, Spain (Simancas)*, Volume 1, 1558-1567, n. 318.

[8] Ibid.

[9] *Calendar of State Papers, Spain (Simancas)*, Volume 2, 1568-1579, n. 431.

[10] Historian Retha M. Warnicke discussed and dispelled the myth of Lettice's illicit pregnancy in *Wicked Women of Tudor England*, pp. 118-20.

[11] *Calendar of State Papers, Spain (Simancas)*, Volume 3, 1580-1586, n. 343.

[12] *Calendar of State Papers, Domestic Series*, Volume 2, p. 137.

[13] G.B. Harrison, *A Second Elizabethan Journal*, Volume 2, p. 132.

[14] Lucy Aikin, *Memoirs of the Court of Queen Elizabeth*, Volume 2, p. 402.

[15] Tracy Borman, *The Private Life of the Tudors*, p. 2.

[16] Arthur Collins, *Letters and Memorials of State*, Volume 2, p. 174.

CHAPTER 20
"FLOUTING WENCHES"

On 12 February 1590, Elizabeth lost her longest-serving woman, Blanche Parry. Blanche had known Elizabeth since the Queen was a toddler in the silver cradle Blanche rocked in 1533. By the time she died at the ripe old age of eighty-two, Parry was a wealthy woman. In her last will, she made several bequests to her friends and family and left Elizabeth her "best diamond" for remembrance.[1] Everything she had in her life she owed to the Queen, whom she adored and loved as her own daughter. Blanche never married, and she was able to devote her energy solely to serving Elizabeth. She was almost blind when she died, but her mental faculties were unimpaired. Blanche was the only living woman who had known Elizabeth since her childhood and offered a precious link to the Queen's past, and her death marked Elizabeth's decline into old age.

It soon became apparent that the gulf between the elderly Queen Elizabeth and her boisterous young maidens was growing wider with each passing year. Whereas in the early years after her accession Elizabeth was adored by her ladies-in-waiting, by the end of her reign she became a figure of ridicule as she turned into a caricature of her former self.

The Queen revelled in the attention of her courtiers, and she deluded herself into believing that everyone still admired her. In fact, people were "weary of an old woman's government".[2]

Elizabeth was becoming more eccentric than ever, and she liked to finagle foreign ambassadors into complimenting her appearance. "Whenever anyone speaks of her beauty she says that she was never beautiful", observed the French ambassador in 1597, adding, "Nevertheless, she speaks of her beauty as often as she can".[3] Elizabeth frequently elicited affirmations of her good looks and made sure that her wrinkled face, ravaged by poisonous makeup, was carefully concealed behind what one historian called "the mask of youth".[4] Painters and miniaturists were forbidden to show the real likeness of the Queen, depicting her instead as the iconic, changeless and radiant Virgin Queen. Elizabeth hated posing for portraits, and "the natural representation of Her Majesty" was forbidden from being painted directly from life. Instead, one officially approved face pattern was produced and inserted into all subsequent portraits.[5] Posing for a portrait took up to three or four hours if the artist was skilled in his craft; the Queen preferred her ladies-in-waiting to be dressed and styled, pretending to be her, instead of sitting in one pose for hours on end.

In her book *The Face of Queenship: Early Modern Representations of Elizabeth I*, Anna Riehl rightly pointed out

"Flouting Wenches"

that Elizabeth's "natural features were highly individual and did not readily fit into a mould of an ideal feminine beauty".[6] These features became distorted as the Queen grew older. In the early years of her long reign, she was often described as way too thin for her tall figure. In 1561, it was reported that she was "extremely thin and the colour of a corpse".[7] The reason Elizabeth was so slender was that she enjoyed physical exercise and ate sparingly. She "never ate meat but when her appetite served her nor drank wine without allaying it [with water]".[8] Elizabeth retained a slim figure throughout her long life, but she gained considerable weight between 1581 and 1597. In 1581, her tailor was paid for altering and enlarging some items of clothing, including thirty pairs of bodices, and in 1596 an eyewitness reported that Elizabeth was "very strongly built".[9] These descriptions are borne out by several miniatures painted by the Queen's favourite court painter, Nicholas Hilliard, who depicted her with a fuller face and incipient double chin.

The reason Elizabeth gained weight was that she had a notorious sweet tooth and enjoyed eating sugar in all forms and shapes, a rarity imported from the New World and reserved for the upper classes. Eating large amounts of sugar on a daily basis made the Queen's teeth discoloured and unequal. The French ambassador who saw her in 1597 recorded that some of Elizabeth's teeth were missing "so that

Great Ladies

one cannot understand her easily when she speaks quickly".[10] Ever since she started overindulging in sugar, Elizabeth began suffering from recurring tooth pain. In 1577, for instance, it was reported that "the Queen was in some part of this year under excessive anguish by pains of her teeth insomuch that she took no rest for divers nights, and endured very great torment night and day".[11] Elizabeth was terribly afraid of the procedure of tooth extraction since it was painful and did not guarantee a successful outcome.

By the time she reached her sixties, Elizabeth was bald, having only wisps of her natural grey hair hanging to her shoulders when she was not wearing elaborate wigs. The skin on her wrinkled face, often painted with a toxic mixture of white lead and vinegar, was dry and deathly pale. Yet the Queen enjoyed showing herself off in her finest gowns, jewel-encrusted wigs and loaded with heavy necklaces made of large pearls and gemstones. Elizabeth, who retained her "vigorous disposition", often appeared grotesque in her voluminous gowns and excessive ornaments.[12] She was loath to acknowledge that she grew older and weaker. "Age in itself is a sickness", she once mused in a conversation with her much-favoured godson, John Harrington.[13] Women, who knew what was happening behind closed doors, often ridiculed and poked fun at their royal mistress. They often laughed at Elizabeth for "trying to play the part of a woman still young".[14] Indeed,

"Flouting Wenches"

Elizabeth tried to pretend that she was young and attractive and often danced, walked tirelessly in her gardens and stomped her feet at bad news. Elizabeth Talbot, Countess of Shrewsbury, better known as Bess of Hardwick, told Mary Queen of Scots that she would never return to court to attend Elizabeth because she was afraid of her when she was in a rage. Bess also recounted how her daughter, Mary Talbot, could not cease to "laugh up her sleeve" at the old Queen. Bess herself was no better; she and her friend Margaret Douglas, Countess of Lennox, could not look at each other while in the Queen's presence "for fear of bursting into gales of laughter".[15]

Elizabeth's waning beauty and health problems rendered her grumpy and unbearable. She demanded high moral standards from her youthful attendants, but they carried out indiscreet love affairs just under the Queen's nose. Some of her ladies eloped to marry in secret while other clandestine marriages were discovered only after ladies were unable to conceal their pregnancies. The Queen, who suppressed her own romantic feelings for Robert Dudley, had no inclination to tolerate blatant disregard of her authority and had no compunction about beating, slapping or raging against any girl who offended her.

The Queen could be merciless in punishing her ladies, but some, like the audacious Mary Howard, deserved chiding. One day she appeared at court wearing a rich velvet gown

Great Ladies

"powdered with gold and pearl". The Queen was envious because she thought that Mary was dressed richer than she herself. A few days later, Elizabeth ordered her servant to bring her Mary's gown and donned it herself. It was a pathetic sight because the gown was "far too short for Her Majesty's height". Elizabeth teased her ladies, asking them what they thought of her new dress. When the Queen saw that none of her ladies came forth with a reply, she asked Mary Howard if the gown was "not made too short, and ill becoming?" Mary, abashed, agreed. "If it become not me, as being too short, I am minded it shall never become thee, as being too fine; so it fitteth neither well" was the Queen's conclusion. The indecorous dress was stored away, never to be worn by Mary Howard during Elizabeth's lifetime, and the maid herself was "abashed at this sharp rebuke".[16]

As Elizabeth aged, the question of who would succeed England's Virgin Queen was asked more frequently than ever. King James VI of Scotland, son of the executed Mary Queen of Scots, was the most likely successor. Elizabeth's courtiers "adored him as the rising sun, and neglected her as being now ready to set".[17] Just like her half sister, Mary, Elizabeth was buried alive by her fickle courtiers, who were now weary of the Virgin Queen's longevity and flocked to James's side.

Knowing the constant speculation upon her mortality, Elizabeth would many times observe wryly that she was

"Flouting Wenches"

"mortua non sepulta", dead but not yet buried. Yet, as if out of spite, she tried to prove to her courtiers that she was not ready to satisfy them and drop dead. The physical activity she liked so much kept her fit, and she remained agile until the end. In 1597, when she was sixty-four, the French ambassador observed that it was "a strange thing to see how lively she is in body and mind, and nimble in everything she does".[18] Five years later a visitor to Oatlands Palace saw her "walking as freely as if she had been only eighteen years old".[19] By that time she danced rarely, but in February 1600 she danced energetically to "show that she is not so old as some would have her".[20] She rode on horseback and hunted late into her sixties, but she often rested for two days after an hour in the saddle.

The old Queen became ever more reliant on her ladies, who, apart from carrying out basic duties, also had to read out private correspondence to Elizabeth, who was no longer able to go through the papers herself. The Queen often acknowledged the efforts of her attendants. In the early 1590s, she took a liking to Bridget Manners, a young maid of honour who was employed in the royal household in November 1592. In a letter to Bridget's mother written shortly after the girl was sworn in, the vice-chamberlain of the Queen's household extolled "the exceeding good modest and honourable behaviour and carriage of my Lady Bridget your daughter".

Bridget's "careful and diligent attendance" prompted the Queen to acknowledge that "she had cause to thank you for her, and you may take comfort of so virtuous a daughter".[21] In the 1590s, when the Queen's maids of honour were secretly getting married behind Elizabeth's back, Bridget seemed like an incarnation of purity, a reminder of a once chaste court of the ageless Gloriana. Yet several years after her appointment, Bridget also married without the Queen's consent and was briefly in disgrace with Elizabeth.

In February 1603, Queen Elizabeth lost yet another lady of the Privy Chamber who served her faithfully for years. Katherine Howard, Countess of Nottingham, was the daughter of Henry Carey and thus Mary Boleyn's granddaughter. The countess was some fourteen years younger than Elizabeth, and when she died, the Queen was beset with grief. Observers noted that Elizabeth took Katherine's death "much more heavily" than the countess's husband, Charles Howard, Lord Admiral. Katherine entered Elizabeth's household as a young girl of twelve, and the two had been inseparable ever since. The countess was appointed as the chief Lady of the Privy Chamber in 1572, and in 1598 she became Groom of the Stool, taking care of the chamber pot.

Elizabeth valued ladies who managed to stay politically neutral, and it seems that Katherine's loyalty was solely to the Queen. No scandal was attached to the countess's name throughout her long service to Elizabeth, but in the seventeenth century, a deathbed confession allegedly made by the countess entered the historical record. The story goes that when the Queen's favourite, the Earl of Essex, was imprisoned in the Tower after he rebelled against her, he sent Elizabeth a ring she had once given him. This gesture was secretly understood between Elizabeth and Essex to mean that they were still on good terms. The boy who was tasked to deliver this ring to Philadelphia Scrope, Katherine Howard's sister, delivered it to Katherine instead. Instead of delivering the ring to Elizabeth, Katherine decided to hide it away. The Queen, who waited for any sign from Essex, signed his death warrant. When the countess told the Queen what she had done, Elizabeth allegedly cried out: "God may forgive you, but I never can!"[22] Historian Susan Doran dismissed this story as a "romantic myth, with no foundation of truth".[23]

When Katherine died on 23 February 1603, the Queen was beset with grief and withdrew from public life. "The Queen loved the Countess well, and hath much lamented her death, remaining ever since in a deep melancholy that she must die herself, and complained of many infirmities wherewith she seemed suddenly to be overtaken", recorded one observer.[24] From that point on, Elizabeth grew weaker and lost the will to live. Her last days were vividly described by one of her maids of honour, Elizabeth Southwell, who

Great Ladies

remained with the Queen until the end. Elizabeth Southwell was sworn in as maid of honour in 1599. One observer remarked: "The young fair Mistress Southwell shall this day be sworn Maid of Honour. My Lady Newton sought it for her daughter."[25] Southwell was eminently suitable to become the Queen's servant—she was young, good-looking and had ties to the most prominent of Elizabeth's ladies. She was the Queen's kinswoman and goddaughter and a granddaughter of Katherine Howard, Countess of Nottingham. The female members of her family served in the royal household for decades; her paternal grandmother, for instance, served as one of Queen Mary's maids in the 1550s.

According to Southwell's testimony, the Queen surrounded herself with her Boleyn relatives. Philadelphia Scrope was chief among the women who were with the Queen as she slipped into decline. Scrope was Elizabeth's "near kinswoman" and "very private" with her; she was a highly esteemed Lady of the Bedchamber.[26] A portrait of Philadelphia shows her holding a comb that belonged to Elizabeth's mother, Anne Boleyn—perhaps the Careys owned more mementoes that belonged to Anne and were thus a precious link to Elizabeth's past.

In her final illness, Elizabeth refused to take to bed, eat or accept medical help. When Charles Howard, widower of Katherine, Countess of Nottingham, was summoned to the

"Flouting Wenches"

Queen's side, he encouraged her to rest in bed instead of sitting motionlessly on the floor among her cushions with a finger constantly in her mouth. It was believed that he would be able to persuade the Queen to rest, but Elizabeth "said softly to him if he had known what she had seen in her bed he would not persuade her as he did".[27] The Lord Admiral had at least managed to convince Elizabeth to eat some broth, but the Queen complained that she felt as if "tied with a chain of iron about my neck". Two of her ladies discovered a queen of hearts playing card "with an iron nail knocked through the head of it" underneath Elizabeth's chair. The ladies were afraid to remove the card, "thinking it to be some witchcraft".[28] In reality, it was not witchcraft that killed Elizabeth, as the Queen was troubled with a "sore throat" as well as "heat in her breasts and dryness in her mouth and tongue" caused by a combination of tonsillitis and flu.[29]

On 23 March 1603, Elizabeth became speechless and communicated with her prelates and courtiers only by gestures. The Queen kept her divines on their knees for hours, and when the elderly Archbishop of Canterbury wanted to get up, Elizabeth gestured for him to stay and pray for her. Interpretation of the Queen's gestures was left to Philadelphia Scrope, who learned their meanings while constantly attending her royal mistress. She was among the intimate group of women who attended Elizabeth when the prelates left the Queen's bedchamber.[30] It was Lady Scrope who informed her brother, Sir Robert Carey, that Queen Elizabeth died between two and three in the morning of 24 March 1603.

As soon as Carey learned about it, he went into the coffer chamber, where maids of honour slept, and found "all the ladies weeping bitterly". His sister, Lady Scrope, gave him a ring she received from James of Scotland; Carey was to present it to the King as proof that Elizabeth was dead. Carey galloped off for Scotland and reached Edinburgh on 26 March 1603 to inform James that he was, at last, King of England. He was henceforward known as James I of England.[31]

If Lady Philadelphia Scrope believed that the new Queen would favour her and the ladies who spent large parts of their lives tirelessly serving Queen Elizabeth, she was mistaken. The twenty-nine-year-old Anne of Denmark, James I's wife, "showed no favour to the elderly ladies but to Lady Rich and such like company".[32] Lady Penelope Rich had long been living in an adulterous relationship with Lord Mountjoy and had several illegitimate children with him. The moral decline of the early Jacobean court was evident and, as the young maid of honour Anne Clifford remarked with some distaste, "all the Ladies about the Court had gotten such ill names that it was grown a scandalous place".[33]

"Flouting Wenches"

In the words of historian Tracy Borman, the death of Queen Elizabeth "represented more than just the end of the Tudor dynasty. It was the end of a court life to which England had become accustomed, with its clear—if interlinked—distinction between the public and private life of the monarch".[34] The end of Elizabeth's reign also marked the decline of women's influence at court. The sole fact that Elizabeth was a female monarch gave the women serving at court an unusual importance. They controlled access to the Queen and were responsible for maintaining the public persona Elizabeth was so eager to protect from her subjects, fashioning herself as a semi-divinity. Never again in the history of England would women wield so much power as they did during the reign of the capricious Virgin Queen.

NOTES

[1] TNA PROB 11/75/180: The Last Will of Blanche Parry.

[2] Louis Montrose, *The Subject of Elizabeth: Authority, Gender, and Representation*, p. 212.

[3] Anna Riehl, *The Face of Queenship*, p. 46.

[4] Roy Strong, *Nicholas Hilliard*, pp. 14-19 and 21-6, and *Artists of the Tudor Court*, pp. 9-13 and 126-32.

[5] George Lillie Craik, *The Pictorial History of England*, p. 550.

[6] Anna Riehl, *The Face of Queenship*, p. 48.

[7] Frederick Chamberlin, *The Private Character of Queen Elizabeth*, pp.51, 56.

[8] Ibid., p. 89.

[9] Janet Arnold, *Queen Elizabeth's Wardrobe Unlock'd*, p. 1.

[10] Ibid., p. 8.

[11] Frederick Chamberlin, *The Private Character of Queen Elizabeth*, p. 67.

Great Ladies

[12] Janet Arnold, *Queen Elizabeth's Wardrobe Unlock'd*, p. 10.

[13] Donna B. Hamilton, *Shakespeare and the Politics of Protestant England,* p. 87.

[14] Tracy Borman, *Elizabeth's Women*, p. 376.

[15] Ibid., p. 314.

[16] *The Ladies' Garland*, Volume 1, p. 314.

[17] William Camden, *The History of the Most Renowned and Victorious Princess Elizabeth*, p. 659.

[18] Louis Montrose, *The Subject of Elizabeth: Authority, Gender, and Representation*, p. 238.

[19] Ibid.

[20] Carolly Erickson, *The First Elizabeth*, p. 403.

[21] *The Manuscripts of His Grace the Duke of Rutland, G.C.B., Preserved at Belvoir Castle*, Volume 1, p. 304-05.

[22] *The Progresses, Processions, and Magnificent Festivities of King James The First, His Royal Consort, Family, and Court*, p. 35

[23] Susan Doran, *The Death of a Friend: Queen Elizabeth I, Bereavement, and Grief,* Oxford University Press's Blog [http://blog.oup.com/2015/03/queen-elizabeth-grief/]

[24] Ibid.

[25] Charlotte Merton, *The Women Who Served Queen Mary and Queen Elizabeth*, p. 39.

[26] Catherine Loomis, *Elizabeth Southwell's Manuscript Account of the Death of Queen Elizabeth I*, p. 485.

[27] Henry Clifford, *The Life of Jane Dormer, Duchess of Feria*, p. 99.

[28] Ibid.

[29] Frederick Chamberlin, *The Private Character of Queen Elizabeth,* p. 75.

[30] Sir Robert Carey, *Memoirs of Robert Carey, Earl of Monmouth*, p. 122.

[31] Ibid., pp. 123-27.

[32] *The Diaries of Lady Anne Clifford* (ed. D.J.H Clifford), p. 36.

[33] Ibid.

[34] Tracy Borman, *The Private Life of the Tudors*, p. 373.

PICTURE SECTION

Greenwich Palace in 1558. Greenwich was one of the main royal residences of the Tudors. Queens Mary and Elizabeth were born there in 1516 and 1533 respectively.

Stained glass at Canterbury Cathedral depicting Elizabeth Woodville and her daughters.

Great Ladies

Cecily of York in a detail from the stained glass at Canterbury Cathedral.

Elizabeth Woodville, wife of Edward IV and mother of Elizabeth of York.

Margaret Beaufort. "My Lady the King's Mother" was a constant presence at her son's court.

Elizabeth of York, the mother of the Tudor dynasty.

Margaret Grey, Dowager Marchioness of Dorset. She served as Elizabeth of York's maid of honour and went on to forge a long and successful career at the Tudor court. She was the paternal grandmother of Lady Jane Grey.

Great Ladies

Katharine of Aragon, Henry VIII's banished first wife.

Picture section

This medal cast in 1534 is the only undisputable likeness of Henry VIII's second wife, the divisive Anne Boleyn.

Margery Horsman by Hans Holbein. Anne Boleyn's maid of honour, who was reluctant to testify against her royal mistress in 1536. Towards the end of her life, Anne developed a "great friendship" with Margery.

Great Ladies

Jane Seymour, Henry VIII's third wife, who died of puerperal fever.

Picture section

An *Unknown Woman* formerly known as Margaret Pole, Countess of Salisbury.

Great Ladies

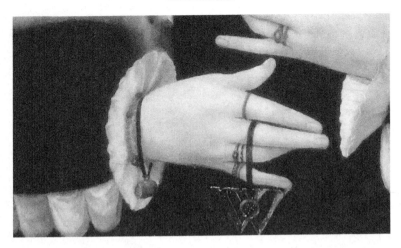

Detail from the portrait of the *Unknown Woman*, formerly labelled as Margaret Pole, Countess of Salisbury. There is no coat of arms or inscription, but the symbolism points to the possibility that this is indeed Margaret. It is believed that the barrel on her bracelet is a subtle reference to her father's execution (George, Duke of Clarence, was drowned in a butt of malmsey wine). The sitter also holds the letter *W*, a reference, perhaps, to her executed brother, the young Earl of Warwick.

Picture section

Anne of Cleves, the unwanted fourth bride of Henry VIII.

Great Ladies

A miniature of an unknown woman, possibly Katherine Howard.

Katherine Parr, Henry VIII's sixth and final wife.

Sketch of an unknown woman by Hans Holbein. This sketch is believed to represent Anne Herbert, Countess of Pembroke, the sister of Henry VIII's sixth wife, Katherine Parr.

Great Ladies

Anne Seymour, Duchess of Somerset, wife of Edward Seymour and aunt by marriage of Edward VI.

Picture section

Effigy of Frances Grey, née Brandon, mother of Lady Jane Grey.

The Execution of Lady Jane Grey, nineteenth-century oil painting by Paul Delaroche.

Great Ladies

Mary Tudor, first English Queen regnant.

Elizabeth Tudor, England's Virgin Queen.

Great Ladies

Katherine Knollys, née Carey, by Steven van der Meulen. She was the daughter of Mary Boleyn and her first husband, William Carey. Her brother, Henry, was rumoured to have been the King's illegitimate son, and Katherine's stunning resemblance to Henry VIII seems to indicate that she, too, may have been a royal bastard. She was much favoured by Queen Elizabeth.

Picture section

Lettice Dudley, née Knollys, Countess of Leicester. Katherine Knollys's daughter and second wife of Robert Dudley, Earl of Leicester. She incurred the wrath of Queen Elizabeth by marrying Dudley, Elizabeth's friend and, some whispered, lover. The Queen dubbed her with the nickname "she-wolf" and never forgave her.

Great Ladies

Blanche Parry's effigy in Bacton Church shows her kneeling in adoration before Queen Elizabeth. Blanche served the Queen since Elizabeth's birth in 1533. Her faithful service ended with Blanche's death on 12 February 1590 at the ripe old age of eighty-two.

Picture section

Katherine Howard, Countess of Nottingham. She was the daughter of Henry Carey and thus Mary Boleyn's granddaughter. The countess was a long-time servant of Queen Elizabeth; her death on 23 February 1603 plunged the elderly Queen into a state of deep melancholy.

SELECTED BIBLIOGRAPHY

Primary sources: Manuscripts

TNA E 101/421/13: The New Year gift roll for 1534.

TNA PROB 11/23/362: Will of Lord William Willoughby, Knight of Willoughby and Eresby.

TNA PROB 11/37/342: Will of Jane Dudley, Duchess of Northumberland of Chelsea, Middlesex.

TNA PROB 11/75/180: Will of Blanche Parry, Gentlewoman of the Queen's Privy Chamber.

TNA SP 1/167/14: The undated letter from Katherine Howard to Thomas Culpeper.

Printed primary sources

Ascham, R. *The Whole Works of Roger Ascham.* John Russel Smith, 1865.

Bietenholz, P.G. *The Correspondence of Erasmus: Letters 842-992 (1518-1519).* University of Toronto Press, 1982.

Brewer, J.S. & Gairdner, J., eds. *Calendar of State Papers, Spain.* Institute of Historical Research (1862-1932).

Brewer, J.S. & Gairdner, J., eds. *Letters and Papers, Foreign and Domestic, of the Reign of Henry VIII.* 28 Volumes. Institute of Historical Research (1862-1932).

Selected Bibliography

Brigden, S. ed. *The Letters of Richard Scudamore to Sir Philip Hoby, September 1549-March 1555.* Camden Miscellany, xxx, (Camden Soc. 4th ser. 39, 1990).

Camden, W. *The History of the Most Renowned and Victorious Princess Elizabeth Late Queen of England.* Flesher, 1688.

Carey, R. *Memoirs of Robert Carey.* Alexander Moring Ltd, 1905.

Cavendish, G. *The Life and Death of Cardinal Wolsey.* S.W. Singer, Harding and Leppard, 1827.

Clifford, H. *The Life of Jane Dormer, Duchess of Feria.* Burns & Oates, 1887.

Dowling, M., ed. *William Latymer's Cronickille of Anne Bulleyne.* Camden Miscellany, xxx (Camden Soc. 4th ser. 39, 1990).

Ellis, H. *Original Letters Illustrative of English History*, Volume 2. (2nd series). Harding and Lepard, 1827.

Everett Wood, A. *Letters of Royal and Illustrious Ladies of Great Britain, Three Volumes.* London: H. Colburn, 1846.

Examination of Queen Katherine Howard in Calendar of the manuscripts of the Marquis of Bath, preserved at Longleat, Wiltshire. Volume 2. John Falconer, 1907.

Foxe, J. *The Actes and Monuments of the Church.* Hobart Seymour, ed. M. Robert Carter & Brothers, 1855.

Giustiniani, S. *Four Years at the Court of Henry VIII.* Two Volumes. Translated by Rawdon Brown. London: Smith, Elder, 1854.

Gough Nichols, J. *The Chronicle of Queen Jane and of Two Years of Queen Mary.* Camden Society, 1850.

Hall, E. *Hall's Chronicle.* J. Johnson, 1809.

Harris, N. *Privy Purse Expenses of Elizabeth of York.* William Pickerint, 1830.
Harris, N. *Testamenta Vetusta. Two Volumes.* Nicholas & Son, 1826.

Great Ladies

Leland, J. *Joannis Lelandi antiquarii de rebus britannicis collectanea.* Richardson, 1770.

Letts, M., ed. *The Travels of Leo of Rozmital.* Hakluyt Society, 2nd ser. 108, 1957.

Mancini, D. *The Usurpation of Richard III.* Clarendon Press, 1969.

More, C. *The Life of Sir Thomas More.* William Pickering, 1828.

Mueller, J., ed. *Katherine Parr: Complete Works and Correspondence.* University of Chicago Press, 2011.

Nichols, J. *A Collection of All the Wills of the Kings and Queens of England.* Society of Antiquaries, 1780.

Pole, R. *Pole's Defense of the Unity of the Church.* Newman Press, 1965.

Sander, N. *Rise and Growth of the Anglican Schism.* Burns and Oates, 1877.

Sharp Hume, M.A. *Chronicle of King Henry VIII of England.* George Bell and Sons, 1889.

St Clare Byrne, M., ed. *The Lisle Letters.* Six Volumes. The University of Chicago Press, 1981.

Wriothesley, C. *A Chronicle of England During the Reigns of the Tudors, from A.D. 1485 to 1559.* Camden Society, 1875.

Selected Bibliography

Secondary sources

Arnold, J. *Queen Elizabeth's Wardrobe Unlock'd*. Maney Publishing, 1988.

Bernard, G.W. *Anne Boleyn: Fatal Attractions*. Yale University Press, 2010.

Bernard, G.W. *The King's Reformation*. Yale University Press, 2007.

Borman, T. *Elizabeth's Women: The Hidden Story of the Virgin Queen*. Vintage, 2010.

Borman, T. *The Private Lives of the Tudors: Uncovering the Secrets of Britain's Greatest Dynasty*. Hodder & Stoughton, 2016.

Chamberlin, F. *The Private Character of Queen Elizabeth*. Dodd Mead & Company, 1922.

Childs, J. *Henry VIII's Last Victim: The Life and Times of Henry Howard, Earl of Surrey*. Thomas Dunne Books, 2007.

Collins, A. *Letters and Memorials of State*. Volume 2. T. Osborne, 1746.

Denny, J. *Anne Boleyn: A New Life of England's Tragic Queen*. Piatkus Books Ltd., 2005.

Doran, S. *Elizabeth I and Her Circle*. Oxford University Press, 2015.

Erickson, C. *The First Elizabeth*. Macmillan, 2007.

Evans, V.S. *Ladies-in-Waiting: Women Who Served at the Tudor Court*. CreateSpace, 2014.

Fox, J. *Jane Boleyn: The True Story of the Infamous Lady Rochford*. Ballantine Books, 2009.

Fraser Tytler, P. *England under the Reigns of Edward VI and Mary*. Richard Bentley, 1839.

Great Ladies

Friedmann, P. *Anne Boleyn: A Chapter of English History, 1527-1536.* Macmillan and Co., 1884.

Furdel Lane, E. *The Royal Doctors, 1485-1714: Medical Personnel at the Tudor and Stuart Courts.* University of Rochester Press, 2001.

Gladish, D.M. *The Tudor Privy Council.* Redford, 1915.

Gunn, S.J. "A Letter of Jane, Duchess of Northumberland in 1553." *English Historical Review 114* (1999): 1267–71.

Hamilton, D.B. *Shakespeare and the Politics of Protestant England.* University Press of Kentucky, 1992.

Harkrider, F.M. *Women, Reform and Community in Early Modern England.* Boydell Press, 2008.

Harris, J.B. *English Aristocratic Women, 1450-1550: Marriage and Family, Property and Careers.* Oxford University Press, 2002.

Head, M.D. *The Ebbs and Flows of Fortune: The Life of Thomas Howard, Third Duke of Norfolk.* University of Georgia Press, 1995.

Hibbert, C. *The Virgin Queen: A Personal History of Elizabeth I.* Tauris Parke Paperbacks, 2010.

Hutchinson, R. *The Last Days of Henry VIII: Conspiracy, Treason and Heresy at the Court of the Dying Tyrant.* Phoenix, 2006.

Ives, E. W. *The Life and Death of Anne Boleyn: The Most Happy.* Blackwell Publishing, 2010.

James, S. *Catherine Parr: Henry VIII's Last Love.* The History Press, 2010.

Kelly, H.A. *The Matrimonial Trials of Henry VIII.* Wipf and Stock Publishers, 2004.
Klarwill, V. *Queen Elizabeth and Some Foreigners.* Bentano's, 1928.

Lipscomb, S. *1536: The Year that Changed Henry VIII.* Lion Hudson, 2009.

Selected Bibliography

Loades, D. *Mary Tudor: A Life*. Basil Blackwell, 1989.

Loomis, C. "Elizabeth Southwell's Manuscript Account of the Death of Queen Elizabeth [with Text]". *English Literary Renaissance*, Vol. 26, No. 3, Monarchs (1996), pp. 482-509.

Medici, C. "More than a Wife and Mother: Jane Dudley, the Woman Who Bequeathed a Parrot and Served Five Queens" in *Scholars and Poets Talk About Queens*, edited by C. Levin and C. Stewart-Nunez. Palgrave MacMillan, 2015.

Merriman, R.B. *Life and Letters of Thomas Cromwell*. Two Volumes. Clarendon Press, 1902.

Montrose, L. *The Subject of Elizabeth: Authority, Gender, and Representation*. University of Chicago Press, 2006.

Myers, A.R. *The Household of Edward IV*. Manchester University Press, 1959.

North, J. *England's Boy King: The Diary of Edward VI, 1547-1553*. Ravenhall, 2005.

Norton, E. *Anne of Cleves: Henry VIII's Discarded Bride*. Amberley Publishing, 2011.

Norton, E. *Bessie Blount: Mistress to Henry VIII*. Amberley Publishing, 2012.

Norton, E. *Jane Seymour: Henry VIII's True Love*. Amberley Publishing, 2010.

Norton, E. *The Boleyn Women: The Tudor Femmes Fatales Who Changed English History*. Amberley Publishing, 2013.

Porter, L. *Katherine the Queen: The Remarkable Life of Katherine Parr*. Macmillan, 2010.

Riehl, A. *The Face of Queenship: Early Modern Representations of Elizabeth I*. Palgrave Macmillan, 2010.

Scarisbrick, J.J. *Henry VIII*. University of California Press, 1968.

Great Ladies

Schofield, J. *The Rise and Fall of Thomas Cromwell: Henry VIII's Most Faithful Servant*. The History Press, 2011.

Smith, Lacey B. *Catherine Howard: The Queen Whose Adulteries Made a Fool of Henry VIII*. Amberley Publishing, 2009.

Soberton, S.B. *Golden Age Ladies: Women Who Shaped the Courts of Francis I and Henry VIII*. CreateSpace, 2016.

Starkey, D. *Elizabeth: The Struggle for the Throne*. Harper Perennial, 2007.

Starkey, D. *Six Wives: The Queens of Henry VIII*. Vintage, 2004.

Stone, J.M. *History of Mary I, Queen of England*. Sands & Co., 1901.

Strong, R. *Artists of the Tudor Court*. Victoria & Albert Museum, 1983.

Tremlett, G. *Catherine of Aragon: Henry's Spanish Queen*. Faber & Faber, 2010.

Varlow, S. "Sir Francis Knollys's Latin Dictionary: New Evidence for Katherine Carey". *Historical Research*, 80 (2007), 315-23.

Walker, G. "Rethinking the Fall of Anne Boleyn". *The Historical Journal*, Vol. 45, No. 1 (Mar., 2002), pp. 1-29.

Warnicke, R.M. *The Rise and Fall of Anne Boleyn: Family Politics at the Court of Henry VIII*. Cambridge University Press, 1991.
Warnicke, R.M. *Wicked Women of Tudor England*. Palgrave MacMillan, 2012.

Weir, A. *Elizabeth of York: A Tudor Queen and Her World*. Ballantine Books, 2013.

Weir, A. *Mary Boleyn: "The Great and Infamous Whore"*. Vintage, 2011.

Weir, A. *The Lady in the Tower: The Fall of Anne Boleyn*. Vintage, 2010.

Selected Bibliography

Weir, A. *The Six Wives of Henry VIII.* Vintage, 2007.

Whitelock, A. *Elizabeth's Bedfellows: An Intimate History of the Queen's Court.* Bloomsbury Publishing, 2013.

Whitelock, A. *Mary Tudor: England's First Queen.* Bloomsbury Publishing, 2010.

Wilkinson, J. *Katherine Howard: The Tragic Story of Henry VIII's Fifth Queen.* Hachette UK, 2016.

Williams, P. *Catherine of Aragon: The Tragic Story of Henry VIII's First Unfortunate Wife.* Amberley Publishing, 2013.

Wilson, A. V. *Queen Elizabeth's Maids of Honour and Ladies of the Privy Chamber.* John Lane, 1922.

Wroe, A. *Perkin: A Story of Deception.* Vintage, 2004.

PhD Dissertations

Merton, Ch. The Women who served Queen Mary and Queen Elizabeth: Ladies, Gentlewomen and Maids of the Privy Chamber, 1553–1603. University of Cambridge, 1991.

Walters Schmid, S. Anne Boleyn, Lancelot de Carle, and the Uses of Documentary Evidence. Arizona State University, 2009.

Websites

http://blog.oup.com/2015/03/queen-elizabeth-grief/

http://www.british-history.ac.uk/catalogue

https://archive.org/

www.bl.uk/learning/timeline/item102878.html

Great Ladies

www.eastgrinsteadonline.com/2015/04/26/history-the-mystery-of-dame-katherine-grey/

www.westminster-abbey.org/our history/people/katherine-knollys

Printed in Great Britain
by Amazon